Are you Ready to Put Your Life in ORDER?

Are you Ready to Put Your Life in ORDER?

Estate Planning Workbook

Donna M. Stifter & Sharon M. Lerz

Copyright © 2012 by Donna M. Stifter & Sharon M. Lerz.

Library of Congress Control Number:		2012912965
ISBN:	Hardcover	978-1-4771-4658-3
	Softcover	978-1-4771-4657-6
	Ebook	978-1-4771-4659-0

All rights reserved. No part of this book may be reproduced or transmitted in any form or by any means, electronic or mechanical, including photocopying, recording, or by any information storage and retrieval system, without permission in writing from the copyright owner.

This book was printed in the United States of America.

To order additional copies of this book, contact:
Xlibris Corporation
1-888-795-4274
www.Xlibris.com
Orders@Xlibris.com

Table of Contents

Chapter 1	**Introduction**	9
	The Unthinkable	12
	Why Hire an Estate Planner?	14
	Gathering Information	15
Chapter 2	**Estate Planning**	17
	Everyone Needs An Estate Plan	19
	Estate Planning Checklist	21
Chapter 3	**Dying Intestate**	34
Chapter 4	**Wills & Trusts**	37
	Revocable Living Trust	40
	Living Trust vs. Will	41
Chapter 5	**Probate**	44
	Duties of the Executor	46
	Avoiding Probate	47
Chapter 6	**Power of Attorney**	48
Chapter 7	**Gathering Personal Documents**	51
	Worksheets	53
Chapter 8	**Biographical Information**	55
Chapter 9	**Insurance**	59
	Life Insurance	61
	Personal Health Insurance Documents	62
	Long Term Care Insurance	64
	Insurance Worksheets	65

Chapter 10	**Home Ownership** 69
	The Different Home Ownership Documents 71
	Household Inventory Worksheets 73
	Social Security Documents 74
	Real Estate Worksheets 75
Chapter 11	**Personal Property** 78
	Credit Card Information Worksheets 80
	Credit Reporting Agencies 81
	Assets Worksheet 82
	Security Accounts Worksheet 83
	Mutual Funds, Credit Union Stock & Bonds 84
	Vehicle Worksheets 85
Chapter 12	**Household Income** 88
	Retirement Accounts and Pension Plans 90
	Household Income, Employer & Retirement 91
	Partnerships & Joint Ventures Worksheet 92
	Household Expenses Worksheet 93
	Utilities Worksheet 94
	Liabilities Worksheet 95
	Tax Record Worksheet 96
Chapter 13	**Benefits Available for Veterans** 97
	Veterans Administration Centers 101
Chapter 14	**Medical Decisions** 103
	Healthcare Power of Attorney & Directives 106
	Medical Information in the Cards 107
	Additional Form Directory 109
	Health Care Power of Attorney Forms 110
	Living Will Declaration Forms 122
	Donor Registry Enrollment Forms 128
	Do Not Resuscitate Orders 130

Chapter 15	Caring for the Elderly 131
	Medicaid.. 133
	Spousal Impoverishment Rule 135
	Verifications Checklist.. 136
	PASSPORT Program 137
	Available Assistance Worksheet.. 138
	National Academy of Elder Law Attorneys 141
	Biographical Information Worksheet 142
	Wishes After Death 149
Chapter 16	Nursing Home Care 151
Chapter 17	Assisted Living 153
Chapter 18	Planning a Funeral 155
	Obituary Worksheet 158
Chapter 19	In Review 159
Chapter 20	Record Retention 162
Chapter 21	Resources 166
	Contact the Authors 167

Chapter 1

Introduction

INTRODUCTION...

The Estate Planning Workbook will outline the important personal information and documents that should be compiled prior to contacting your *ATTORNEY* or *ESTATE PLANNER*.

Included are worksheets intended to help you gather the information needed to begin the estate planning process, including:

- Will(s)
- Trust(s)
- Power(s) of Attorney
- Biographical family information
- Insurances
- Home Ownership
- Personal Property
- Income & Expenses
- Veterans Directives
- Medical & Healthcare Directives
- Basic Medicaid information
- Care of the Elderly
- Assisted Living & Nursing Homes
- Final Memorial Instructions
- Closing your Estate

IT IS NEVER TOO SOON to prepare for the unexpected. Creating your will or trust today gives you the opportunity to choose an executor to handle your estate and personal property. You can also decide who will provide custodial care for minors or the disabled and express your final wishes for memorial services.

This information has been compiled to meet the needs of estate planning in the state of Ohio, specifically in the Geauga County area. If you're not an Ohio resident, other information may be necessary to meet your state's requirements. These requirements can be obtained by contacting your state's Department of Job and Family Services, local senior centers, or state law offices.

Most importantly, as you begin the estate planning process, contact an *ATTORNEY* or *ESTATE PLANNER* to guide you through the process. They are qualified to handle the final planning of your personal property based on the laws of the state and can better protect you and your family both LEGALLY and FINANCIALLY with the proper information.

The following is dedicated to our children, grandchildren and great grandchildren. They are our inspiration for not only preparing this workbook, but for all we do in life. It is with their support and love that we strive to create this workbook as a tool for them and all others to plan ahead, protecting both themselves and their families from being unprepared in the face of unexpected tragedy.

Are You Ready To Put Your Life In Order?

Written by Donna M. Stifter and Sharon M. Lerz

WHAT WOULD YOU DO WHEN THE UNTHINKABLE HAPPENS?

A few hours of preparation today could save you and your family from the daunting job of trying to cope with the death of a loved one while assembling the important personal and health information needed in accordance with estate planning. When tragedy strikes, those affected may not have the ability to do the research required to making truly informed decisions regarding the best course of immediate action needed in the present situation.

Years ago my father was hospitalized, and upon his release, he was not well enough to care for himself. The hospital's social worker suggested he be taken to a nursing home. My mother felt tremendous guilt over the situation and made the emotional decision to take him home and care for him herself. She didn't understand the consequences of that choice. After all, her and my father had been together for over 50 years. Within a few days she realized the level of care he needed was much more than she could handle, even with the help of the family. Although she was an extremely strong woman, caring for her husband was emotionally and physically exhausting.

She quickly realized that entrusting his care to the nursing home would have been the better choice, as he would have qualified for Medicaid at the time. But by taking him home, even for a few days, she now had to pay for his first month in the nursing home out of pocket before applying for Medicaid. The costly fees of the nursing home depleted their entire joint savings, leaving her with her home, a car, and just six dollars in her savings account. For an average, hard working couple living month-to-month on a very fixed income, the financial blow was almost incomprehensible.

While most people believe stories like this could never happen in their own family, they are an all-to-common occurrence.

Are you Ready to Put Your Life in Order?

This book will serve as a guide to all families with estates of all sizes. Planning your estate ahead not only brings peace of mind, but also insures that your family will be able to carry out your own personal wishes. This tool will help you gather the information and records necessary for your attorney or estate planner as they direct you toward the proper plan to fit you and your family's needs.

—Donna M. Stifter

WHY SHOULD AN ATTORNEY OR ESTATE PLANNER PREPARE YOUR WILL, TRUSTS, AND HEALTH PLANS?

Here are a few important reasons:

1. They can better prepare the proper Will or Trust to fit your needs.
2. There are different forms of Trusts, and they can select the one best suited for you and your family's needs.
3. They can arrange an estate plan that may help to avoid probate.
4. They may be able to cut the amount of taxes you will pay, preserving more of your estate for your family.
5. In the event your child passes away, they can arrange for your grandchildren to receive their portion of the estate.
6. They can help you choose a caretaker to look after children who are under the age of eighteen or disabled, and establish the finances needed for their care.
7. They can aid in establishing healthcare directives like living will, durable powers of attorney, donor registration, and Do Not Resuscitate (DNR) or DNR Comfort Care.

WHEN GATHERING INFORMATION...

These are a few questions you may want to think about when you're gathering your personal information and assessing your need for a will, pour-over will, living will, trust, durable power of attorney, etc.

1. Do you have information regarding your family history together, both past and present?
2. Do you have a prenuptial agreement?
3. Which would better for your situation: a will, a revocable estate trust, or both? Do we need a pour-over will? The workbook will better explain these options later. Keep in mind the type of estate plan to best fit your family's needs could be better explained by your attorney or estate planner.
4. Who would be best suited to raise your children or handicapped family members after your gone?
5. Who is the active spouse that manages the family's affairs (wife, husband, or both)?
6. How should your assets be divided after death? Should everything go to the spouse? What percentage will go to the spouse? What percentage will be divided amongst the children?
7. If your spouse is unable to manage the finances, who should be appointed to manage them for him or her?
8. If either spouse is ever unable to make his or her own healthcare decisions, who should make those decisions? One of the children, a caregiver, someone else?
9. Have you gathered all the documents needed for the real estate and business holdings in your possession?
10. Do you have all the information regarding your bank accounts, life insurance policies, automobiles and other recreational vehicles, and any other personal items of value you've acquired?
11. Do you have all the information regarding your mortgages, loans, etc.?
12. Do you have complete records on family income and other expenses like insurance (personal and health), medication, and any other health-related expenses?
13. Have you complied all of your expenses for utilities like heat, electricity, and telephones?

Expenses to consider:

- Living expenses like food, clothing, television programming, etc.
- Taxes (federal, state and city)
- Personal property and real estate
- Titles, insurance, and maintenance for automobiles and other recreational vehicles

Now that you're thinking about the important information and documents necessary look into making an appointment with an attorney or estate planner to complete your ESTATE PLAN and protect yourself and your family.

CHAPTER 2

Estate Planning

ESTATE PLANNING

Some people may feel an estate plan is unnecessary because they haven't accumulated enough wealth to make a plan worthwhile. Sentiments like this are a potentially costly mistake.

A well-planned estate includes not only your personal wishes and needs, but also plans for loved ones in the event you are disabled or incapacitated. It also provides an outline for your financial strategies, healthcare plans, and final instructions like burial and memorial services.

If your health is failing you can express your healthcare wishes through advanced directives with a healthcare power of attorney, living will declaration, organ donation, or DNR order. Without these directives you leave important decisions to your loved ones and a medical staff. These decisions can take an emotional and financial toll on your family.
The following pages will help you gather the information you'll need to set up your estate plan.

EVERYONE NEEDS A PROPER ESTATE PLAN

The following presents some of the typical problems you could face without proper planning. Problems like these can create a burden on the family members left behind to handle your estate.

Without an estate plan there could be a **FINANCIAL BURDEN** on your family, including the costs of probate fees, administrator fees handled by your executor, attorney fees, estate taxes, death taxes, and more. Failure to effectively plan increases the financial burden on your loved ones.

Another problem stemming from lack of preparation lies in **ESTATE ASSETS,** specifically in these areas:

LIQUIDITY: Liquidity refers to the ability to convert an asset into cash quickly. Without planning, you may find you don't have enough liquidity to pay the debts, taxes, costs, expenses and fees necessary.

CASH FLOW: Failure to plan your estate could also result in insufficient income and/or assets to care for loved ones left behind.

TRANSFER OF ASSETS: Without planning, your estate assets could be subject to probate delays and expenses. An effective plan allows for outright transfer of assets to care for minors and/or disabled family members.

Without proper directives, arranging a transfer of care for minors or the disabled can become unnecessarily complicated. The guardian selected by a third party may not be the person you would have chosen, and may not be capable of fulfilling the needs of your loved ones. In addition, an unqualified person may be put in charge of managing the assets left behind in the best interest of your family.

MEDICAL CARE:

A. Who will make decisions on your behalf if you become incapacitated?
   1. Advanced directive and durable power of attorney for healthcare
   2. Living will
   3. HIPPAA release
   4. Mental health proxy

Proper estate planning can eliminate or reduce these problems.

ESTATE PLANNING CHECKLIST: THE BASIC STEPS

STEP ONE: Carefully choose your estate planning team based on personal needs.
　　　_____ A. Attorney
　　　_____ B. Life Underwriter
　　　_____ C. Accountant
　　　_____ D. Trust Officer
　　　_____ E. Charitable Officer
　　　_____ F. Financial Planner

STEP TWO: Gather information and compile a few important lists.
　　　_____ A. Create a list of family members' names, ages, etc.
　　　_____ B. What are your assets and liabilities?
　　　_____ C. List the desired heirs of your estate.
　　　_____ D. What do you hope to gain by planning your estate today?

STEP THREE: If you died today, what would happen?
　　　_____ A. What would happen to your estate?
　　　_____ B. What about your occupation or business?
　　　_____ C. What would happen to your family?

STEP FOUR: Review your answers with your estate planning team.

STEP FIVE: Implement your personalized plan.
　　　_____ A. Does your will(s) and/or trust(s) fit your needs?
　　　_____ B. Do you need a healthcare power of attorney or directive?
　　　_____ C. Have you purchased the necessary insurance?
　　　_____ D. Have you made the proper changes to your investments?

STEP SIX: Review your plan every year.

Your lives are constantly changing and your estate plan should change with it!

INFO SHEET & CHECKLIST

Name: _____
Date if Birth: _____ Social Security #: _____
Spouse Name: _____
Date of Birth: _____ Social Security #: _____
Residence Address: _____
Spouse's Address (if different): _____
Name of Child: _____
   Date of Birth: _____ Social Security #: _____
   Marital Status: _____ Number of Children: _____
Name of Child: _____
   Date of Birth: _____ Social Security #: _____
   Marital Status: _____ Number of Children: _____

CHECKLIST

Yes No
___ ___ Do you and your spouse have updated wills?
___ ___ Have you discussed your estate plans with your family?
___ ___ Have you consulted an estate-planning professional?
___ ___ Have you reviewed the ownership of your assets to determine which are solely owned and which are jointly owned?
___ ___ Do you have a retirement plan?
___ ___ Will your estate have enough worth to both pay bills and provide adequately for your family?
___ ___ Do you know approximately how much you will receive in social security payments upon retirement?
___ ___ Have you designated anyone to handle your affairs if you become incapable of doing so?
___ ___ Have you made arrangements for your long-term care?
___ ___ Have you made arrangements for the long-term care of your dependents?
___ ___ Have you taken any steps to reduce current income taxes and death taxes on your estate?

Are you Ready to Put Your Life in Order?

___ ___ If you own a business, have you consulted a professional to plan for that business's future?

If you checked "No" to any of these questions you better get busy and plan now to protect yourself and your loved ones. Let's get to work!

ESTATE PLANNING INFORMATION

FOR

_____

IMPORTANT ESTATE 　A. Durable Power of Attorney
DOCUMENTS::　　　　B. Will or Trust or Both
　　　　　　　　　　C. Living Will Declaration
　　　　　　　　　　D. Durable Power of Attorney
　　　　　　　　　　　　For Health Care

LEGAL & FINANCIAL ADVISORS:
Name _____
Address _____ City _____ State _____
Zip _____ Phone _____ Cell Phone_____
　　　　　　Fax _____ Email _____

1. Attorney-In-Fact
   Name:_____
       (*Note: usually Husband is for wife and Wife is for Husband*)

2. Alternate Attorney-In-Fact:
   Name _____ Relationship _____
   Address _____ City _____ State _____
   Zip _____ Phone _____ Cell Phone _____
   　　　　　　Fax _____ Email_____

Second Alternate Attorney-in-fact:
   Name _____ Relationship_____
   Address _____ City_____ State_____
   Zip_____Phone_____ Cell Phone_____
   　　　　　　Fax _____ Email _____

Are you Ready to Put Your Life in Order?

LOCATION OF THE FOLLOWING

SAFE DEPOSIT BOX: (if applicable)
    Institution Name _____
    Address _____
    Phone _____ Email _____

Additional important documents:

1. Birth certificates, death certificates, or both
2. Marriage license and any other legal papers
3. Income tax records
4. Military papers

Other possible forms include financial analyses, documents regarding to your residence or automobiles, medical papers, and funeral arrangements.

In Case of Emergency Contact:
    Name _____
    Address _____
            _____
    Phone _____ Fax _____
    Alternate Phone # _____
    Email Address _____

Physician:
    Name _____
    Firm Name _____
    Address _____
            _____
    Phone _____ Fax _____
    Email Address _____

Dentist
    Name _____
    Firm Name _____

Address _____

Phone _____ Fax _____
Email Address _____

Clergy:
   Clergy's Name _____
   Church/Synagogue _____
   Address _____

   Phone _____ Fax _____
   Email Address _____

Legal & Financial Advisor(s): (ie: Attorney/Accountant)
   Name _____
   Firm Name _____
   Address _____

   Phone _____ Fax _____
   Email Address: _____

Executor/Executrix:
   Name _____
   Firm Name _____
   Address _____

   Phone _____ Fax _____
   Email Address: _____

Stock Broker:
   Name _____
   Firm Name _____
   Address _____

   Phone _____ Fax _____
   Email Address _____

Are you Ready to Put Your Life in Order?

Insurance Agent(s)
    Name _____
    Firm Name _____
    Address _____
    _____

    Phone: _____ Fax _____
    Email Address _____

Pension or Union Plan:
    Contact Name_____
    Firm Name _____
    Address _____
    _____

    Phone: _____ Fax _____
    Email Address _____

Real Estate Broker:
    Name _____
    Firm Name _____
    Address _____
    _____

    Phone: _____ Fax _____
    Email Address _____

Property Deeds Located:
    _____
    _____
    _____

Safe Deposit Box(es):
    Name of Bank _____
    Box # _____
    Address _____
    _____

    Phone: _____ Fax _____
    Email Address _____
    Key is located _____

Income Tax Records:
Location _____
_____
_____

Present and/or Former Employer(s)
    Contact Name _____
    Company Name _____
    Address _____
    _____

    Phone: _____ Fax _____
    Email Address _____

Funeral Home where Arrangements have been made:
    Contact Name _____
    Company Name _____
    Address _____
    _____

    Phone: _____ Fax _____
    Email Address _____
    Contract Information is Located:
    _____
    _____

Business Interests (Sole Proprietor, Partnership, Corporation, etc.)
    Form of Interest _____
    Name/Type of Business _____
    Owned by _____
    _____

    Address _____
    _____

    Company Phone _____ Fax _____

Financial Institutions:
  Account Type _____ Account # _____
  Contact Name _____
  Company Name _____
  Address _____
  _____
  Phone: _____ Fax _____
  Email Address _____

FAMILY ESTATE PLAN CHECKLIST

1. _____ Family tree with biographical information of the members or the family.

2. Personal Information and Documents (if applicable)

    _____ Birth Certificate(s)   _____ Adoption Records & Certificate(s)

    _____ Copy of Drivers' License(s)   _____ Passport(s) if any

    _____ Military Service Records   _____ Citizenship Papers and/or green Card

    _____ Cohabitation Agreement   _____ Prenuptial or Post-Nuptial Agreement

    _____ Marriage Certificate   _____ Domestic Partner Registration

    _____ Child and/or Spousal Support   _____ Divorce Decree

                                                            _____ Spouse Remarried

    _____ Contract with Significant other

    _____ Assisted Living Contract   _____ Nursing Home Contract

3. Personal Insurance Documents
    _____ Life Insurance Policies & Companies Information
    _____ Health Insurance Card Copies, Benefits, and Policy Description
    _____ Medicare Card and Benefit Description
    _____ Medicaid Card and Benefit Description
    _____ Medigap or Managed-Care-Organization Policy
    _____ Long-term care Policy
    _____ Long-term Disability Policy

4. Income and Investment Information
    _____ Payroll information, Company, Amount, Etc.
    _____ Information for Checking, Savings accounts

_____ Information for Money Market Account(s)
_____ Certificate of Deposit
_____ Treasuries/Series l/Series EE/Notes
_____ Stock Certificates & Option grant Agreements
_____ Investment Accounts Applications and Agreements
_____ Annuity Contracts
_____ List of Additional Assets, etc.

5. Credit Card Information
   _____ Up-to-date Copies of Credit Report(s)
   _____ Copies of your Active Credit Cards (front and back)
   _____ Copies of Letters Regarding to Closed Credit Cards

6. We need to collect the information and Social Security cards & Documents
   _____ Copies of Social Security Cards (personal, spouse, children)
   _____ Annual Social Security Statement(s)
   _____ Checks of Paid Self-Insurance Taxes

7. Home Ownership Documents

_____ Deeds	_____ Promissory Note(s)
_____ Homeowner's Insurance	_____ Co-Ownership Property Agreement
_____ Fire Insurance	_____ Copy of Survey

   _____ Copy of Title Policy (Warranty
   _____ Rental Agreement of Home or Apartment
   _____ Rent's Insurance
   _____ Appraisals and Evaluation of Property

8. Personal Property
   _____ Appraisals of all valuable items (art, antiques, jewelry, clothing, etc.)

9. Automobiles and Other Recreational Vehicles
   _____ Automobile Title(s) and/or Leases   _____ Boat Title(s)

_____ Automobile Insurance Policy(s)
_____ Boat Insurance Policy(s)
_____ Automobile Loan Document(s)
_____ Boat Loan Document(s)
_____ Recreational Vehicle Title(s)
_____ Recreational Vehicle Insurance Policy(s)
_____ Recreational Vehicle Loan Document(s)

10. Now we have our Retirement Plan Documents
    _____ Type of Pension Plan, Lump sum, monthly, etc.
    _____ Pension Plan summary, description, Annual plan statement, and Annual individual Pension Benefit Statement
    _____ Money/Purchase/Profit-Sharing Plan documents
    _____ Beneficiary designation
    _____ Retirement Account Withdrawal

11. Tax Records
    _____ Tax Returns (for the past three years)
    _____ Medical Expenses
    _____ Investment Expenses
    _____ Employee Business Travel and Entertainment Expenses
    _____ Student Loan Interest Payments
    _____ Real Estate, Taxes, Mortgage Interests, Closing Costs

12. Final Documents for Your Estate Plan
    _____ Advance Directives and Durable Power of Attorney for Healthcare
    _____ Financial Durable Power of Attorney
    _____ Your Wills
    _____ Revocable Living Trust
    _____ Pour Over Will
    _____ Irrevocable Trust
    _____ Contract for Funeral and/or Memorial Arrangements
    _____ Cemetery and/or Funeral Expenses

EVERYONE NEEDS A WILL!

A will outlines where you want your assets to be distributed when you die. It also allows you to name the guardians for your children. And the benefits don't end there . . .

Dying without a will can be a **COSTLY** mistake.

CHAPTER 3

Dying Intestate

WHAT DOES IT MEAN TO DIE INTESTATE?

Dying intestate refers to dying without a will. This means there is no official plan as to where your money and personal property will be distributed, no guardian appointed to care for your children, and the list goes on . . .

Who would make the decision if there is no will?

The judgment will be left up to the probate court, a division of the common pleas court. The probate court sees that all debts, taxes, and financial affairs of the deceased are left to those legally entitled to receive them.

Handling an Estate WITHOUT A WILL:

1. The probate court will appoint an executor of the estate to work with the court and see that the decedents financial affairs are resolved and the remainder of the estate is distributed according to the instructions spelled out by the probate court.
2. There will be an administrator appointed by the probate court for the estate. Ohio law requires the surviving spouse of the decedent to be appointed as the administrator. If there is no spouse or the spouse declines, the court will appoint the next of kin. And if there is no next of kin, the courts will appoint another person deemed suitable. The administrator must be a resident of the state in which the deceased lived.

What is an Administrator?

1. Before the court officially recognizes the administrator, this person must sign a letter of appointment that spells out the administrative duties. If the administrator doesn't fulfill these duties faithfully, the court can issues fines or even select a new administrator.
2. The administrator must post a bond paid for by the decedent's estate. This covers any potential losses the estate might suffer due

to error or mishandling of the assets during as the administrator's duties are performed.
3. The administrator serving has serious legal responsibilities and could be exposed to financial liabilities if the assets and property are not handled properly.
4. An attorney trained in legal advice should be appointed to provide professional judgments to the administrator in order to make the best decisions and avoid potential problems.

The Responsibilities of the Administrator:

Take inventory of the financial assets and property owned by the deceased at the time of death, which is filed with probate court.

List probate assets—the official term given to assets controlled by the will.

List non-probate assets for tax purposes. These are jointly owned assets do not have to be included in the inventory filed with the court. Non-probate assets are passed on to the co-owners, or beneficiaries.

See that debts are paid. These are debts to creditors, property maintenance costs, local, state and federal taxes, hospital and funeral expenses, probate court costs, bond premiums, appraiser fees, attorney fees, etc.

Make sure the balance of the remaining estate is distributed to the heirs of the deceased.

CHAPTER 4

Wills & Trusts

WILLS AND TRUSTS...

What's the Difference?

WILL:

A legal document setting forth plans for the dispossession of your estate following your death. It also allows you to choose an executor to handle your estate, and provides information as to your income, debts and other expenses. The will even allows you to choose the guardian of any underage children or handicapped persons for which you are responsible.

TRUST:

A legal instrument created to hold and manage your property as well as your tangible and intangible personal property. Putting those assets into a trust transfers them from your ownership to the ownership of the entity known as the trustee. The trustee holds the trust property for the benefit of a beneficiary.

   A. Trusts have a few important advantages that wills don't have:

- They manage your property for you while you are still alive.
- They can reduce your taxes, although it depends on the laws of your state.
- They easily transfer your assets to beneficiaries after your death.
- They allow you more flexibility in how you dispose of your assets.
- They may allow you to avoid probate, saving time and expenses.
- They protect your privacy; unlike a will trusts are not filed and therefore open to public scrutiny

   B. Certain people can benefit greatly from a trust:

     (1) Children under the age of 18—Minors unable to manage money as an adult.

(2) Spendthrift children—Children of any age thought to be unable to manage money properly.
(3) Retirement Management—A trust can be setup to manage your funds during retirement.
(4) Tax Planning—Trusts can act as a tax avoidance; a welcome benefit of any estate plan.
(5) Charitable Trust—The philanthropically inclined may want to establish a trust, or you can contribute to a charity trust already established.

POUR-OVER WILL

A poor-over will is used in conjunction with a trust. This form of will "pours" any property owned by the deceased at the time of death into a trust set up by the person during his or her life.

Some individuals may choose not to put all of their property and assets into trusts during their lifetimes. This may be to avoid the inconveniences that come with buying or selling certain types of property protected by a trust.

REVOCABLE LIVING TRUST...

A Revocable Living Trust gives you the freedom to sell, spend or give away your assets while you're still alive. The trust's condition can be changed to fit your personal situation.

A Revocable Living Trust can be an important part of your estate plan. While it may not fit everyone's situation, a few of its features are notable:

1. Assets in the trust pass to the trust beneficiaries outside of probate, saving time, money, and possible complications.
2. The creator can serve as the trustee or select another to serve as trustee.
3. An alternate trustee can serve when the trust creator is no longer capable.

The revocable trust does not have any special tax advantages, since all income is taxed to the creator and the assets are subject to federal estate taxes upon the creator's death.

IRREVOCABLE LIVING TRUST

This form of trust allows you to gift personal property while you're still alive. That gift is then subject to a federal gift tax paid by the gift-giver. You forfeit all control of it in order to receive an exemption from federal estate taxes. You better be careful, once this trust is established, it is impossible to revise.

LIVING TRUST VS. WILL . . .

What are the advantage and disadvantages?

	Will	**Trust**
Avoids Probate	No	Yes
Saves on Taxes	Yes	Yes
Protection If Incapacitated	No	Yes
Costs	Less Costly	More Costly

Many people favor using the traditional will due to its familiarity and maintainability. However individuals with privacy concerns and a preference to avoid probate should consider choosing a living trust. Individual circumstances should dictate whether a will or a trust is more beneficial. In some cases, you may want both a will and a trust.

Please note . . .

Whenever you're making important decisions in the estate planning process, it is always best to consult an attorney or estate planner.

LAST WILL AND TESTAMENT

I, _____, the Testator, sign my name to this instrument this _____ day of _____, _____, and being first duly sworn, do hereby declare to the undersigned authority that I sign and execute this instrument as my Will and that I sign it willingly, in the presence of the undersigned witnesses, that I execute it as my free and voluntary act for the purpose expressed in the Will, and that I am eighteen years of age or older, of sound mind, and under no constraint or undue influence.

Testator Signature: _____

We, _____ and _____
And _____, the witnesses, sign our names to this instrument, being first duly sworn, and do hereby declare to the undersigned authority that the Testator signs and executes this instrument as the Testator's will and that the Testator signs it willingly in our presence, and that the Testator executes it as the Testator's free and voluntary act for the purposes expressed in the will, and that each of us, in the presence and hearing of the Testator, at the Testator's request, and in the presence of each other, hereby signs this will, on the date of the instrument, as witness to the Testator's signing, and that to the best of our knowledge the Testator is eighteen years of age or older, of sound mind and memory, and under no constraint or undue influence, and the witnesses are of adult age and otherwise competent to be witnesses.

Witness Signature: _____

    Name: _____
    City: _____
    State: _____

Witness Signature: _____

    Name: _____
    City: _____
    State: _____

Witness Signature: _____

    Name: _____
    City: _____
    State: _____

STATE OF OHIO COUNTY OF _____

Subscribed, sworn to and acknowledged before me by _____, the Testator, and subscribed and sworn to before me by _____ and _____ and _____, the witnesses, on this _____ day of _____, _____.

_____
Notary public, or other officer authorized to take and certify acknowledgments and administer oaths.

CHAPTER 5

Probate

PROBATE...

The estate named in your Will is handled by the probate court, which is a part of the state's judicial department There are laws governing the legal procedures of probate court, and these laws often vary from amongst states.

What is the purpose of probate?

Probate refers to the method by which your estate is managed and processed through the legal system after you die. The process is meant to transfer your estate to beneficiaries in an orderly and supervised manner. Steps of probate include swearing in the executor, notifying heirs and creditors of your death, inventorying your property, and distributing the estate to beneficiaries, creditors, tax collectors, and more.

Probate applies to your estate whether or not you have a will, however the process is far smoother when a valid will is involved.

There are costs associated with probate. Some of these costs include court-filing fees associated with the opening of the will, executor fees, and attorney fees. Many of these expenses are necessary, but there are ways to keep costs down. One of the easiest cost-eliminating decisions is choosing a family member as executor. Family members are more likely to administrate the process without compensation.

The next section will give you a brief list as to how you may be able to avoid the probate of your estate. It will also provide a list as to the duties your executor will have to fulfill as administrator of the estate.

DUTIES OF THE EXECUTOR...

Probate court has a primary list of duties the administrator must follow. Keep in mind this list can vary from state to state.

Choosing an executor is a delicate process. This person must have your best interests in mind as well as the interests of your loved ones. The executor is required to follow the laws of probate process, which coincides with the handling of an estate. The following outlines some of the responsibilities.

1. Petition the court to open probate.
2. Petition the court to admit the will.
3. Notify all beneficiaries to the will
4. Notify all creditors of the deceased that probate administration has opened. (This is a legal notice that will run in the local paper.)
5. Obtain a performance bond, paid by the deceased's assets.
6. Inventory the deceased's assets.
7. Seek court approval to sell any assets that may be necessary to pay the debts.
8. See that all debts and state income taxes, federal estate taxes, and state death taxes are paid.
9. Distribute the estate's net assets to beneficiaries according to the will. (If there is no will, the state will settle the estate and make all the decisions.)
10. Once all debts, taxes, and beneficiaries have been paid and assets are distributed the estate will be closed.

Remember this is a general list as to what the executor can expect. The estate might have complications that require additional work.

AVOIDING PROBATE...

There are certain accounts in which you could place your assets that would not be included in the probate of your estate in the event of your death. The catch? You must have a co-owner or beneficiary that survives you. These accounts could be put in a form of ownership, which would be distributed directly to the survivor or beneficiary.

1. Below we have listed a few ways these accounts could be named:
2. Placing the estate in a joint-owners account with right of survivorship.
3. Creating a life estate with remainder interests.
4. Creating a revocable or irrevocable living trust.
5. Having life insurance with a named beneficiary.
6. Placing your assets in annuities with a named beneficiary.
7. Having a pension with a named beneficiary.
8. Any investment accounts you have can be transferred on death (TOD).

CHAPTER 6

Power of Attorney

POWER OF ATTORNEY...

The power of attorney is a document enabling you to appoint an agent to act on your behalf in the event you're unable to do so effectively. There are different forms of powers of attorney that fit different personal situations. Here are four of the most commonly used options:

1. Limited Power of Attorney—Hence the name, this form is the most limited of the powers of attorney. It is primarily used for the one-time transfer or sale of a specific item like a vehicle.
2. General Power of Attorney—This gives the agent full power and authority to perform all acts the grantor would perform if he or she was present. This form of power of attorney may be revoked anytime and is automatically revoked upon the grantor's death.
3. Durable Power of Attorney—Unlike the general power of attorney, the durable power of attorney does not end even in the event the grantor becomes incapacitated. It establishes the agent's right to handle the following circumstances with complete authority:

    a. Handling of all accounts and assets on the grantor's behalf, including a safety deposit and its contents.
    b. Buying or selling of personal, intangible or mixed property.
    c. Exercising the grantor's rights to securities as well as any other rights that may be owned.
    d. Borrowing money, (including any insurance policy loans.)
    e. Purchasing, manage, or sell real property.
    f. Ability to demand, compromise and receive any rights, property (personal, intangible and/or mixed, etc.).
    g. Handling all matters in respect to taxes.
    h. Handling of all legal documents.
    i. Engaging in services needed like legal aid, management, maintenance, and disposition of property.
    j. Obligations to maintain and support the health and well being of the grantor like authorizing medical and surgical procedures.

4. Healthcare Power of Attorney—Grants the agent the authority to make healthcare decisions on the grantor's behalf in the event that person is unable to make the decision. There is no expiration date of this document. It is authorized in the presence of two witness parties. Neither party can be the physician.

Please note . . .

The importance of contacting your **PERSONAL ATTORNEY** or **ESTATE PLANNER** cannot be emphasized enough. These parties are better able to guide you toward the correct power of attorney decision to meet your and your family's needs.

CHAPTER 7

Gathering Personal Documents

START GATHERING YOUR PERSONAL DOCUMENTS...

It's time to begin preparation process and gather all pertinent documents that will not only help you, but also your loved ones, attorney, and estate planner in case of emergency.

Consider protecting this information in a safe place like a lock box, safe, or attorney's office. Keeping everything in one place will allow easy access and the ability to obtain information quickly and accurately. This is especially important if others have to act on your behalf and make quick decisions based on your personal information.

Here we go!

Are you Ready to Put Your Life in Order?

PERSONAL DOCUMENTS

For

_____

Birth Certificate—Official certificate and a copy   _____

Adoption Decree(s)—Certified Copy(s)   _____

Child and/or Spousal Support Contract(s)   _____

Driver's License(s)—(Current Photo Copy)   _____

Passport(s)   _____

Military Record of Service   _____
    Date of Entry, Classifications, Date of separation (Discharge)

Citizenship Records and/or Green Card   _____

Cohabitation Agreement—Stating Financial and General Obligations   _____
    (This is a contract if you are NOT married)

Domestic Partner Registration   _____

Pernupterial Agreement—Contract   _____

Postnuptial Agreement—Contract   _____

Marriage Certificate—Original or Certified Copy   _____

Divorce Decree—Official Certificate or Certified Copy   _____

Death Certificate—Certified Copy   _____

FAMILY RECORDS

Children (own or adopted), Birth date, Residence
_____ _____
_____ _____
_____ _____
_____ _____

Location of Children's Birth Certificate or Adoption Papers
_____ _____
_____ _____
_____ _____
_____ _____

Living Relatives of Wife and their Residences
_____ _____
_____ _____
_____ _____
_____ _____

Living Relatives of Husband and their Residences
_____ _____
_____ _____
_____ _____
_____ _____

Relatives and Friends to be notified:
Name_____ Name_____
Address_____ Address_____

Telephone_____ Telephone_____
Cell phone_____ Cell Phone_____
Email_____ Email_____

CHAPTER 8

Biographical Information

BIOGRAPHICAL INFORMATION

Name_____
(first, middle, last)
Date_____

Address_____ City_____ State____ Zip_____

Telephone_____ Cell_____ Email_____
Fax_____
Number of years lived at present residence_____

Date of Birth_____ Place of Birth_____
City_____ State_____ County_____ Country_____
Citizenship_____

Medical History_____
_____
Medication(s)_____
Pharmacy_____ Address_____ Phone_____

Social Security No._____ Medicare_____ Medicaid_____

Education_____

Religious Affiliation_____ Church_____
Address_____ City_____ State_____

Occupation_____ Date of Employment_____
Date of Retirement_____

Marital Status_____

Father's Name_____ Date of Birth_____
Place of Birth_____
Deceased_____ Internment_____
Medical History_____

56

Are you Ready to Put Your Life in Order?

Mother's Name_____ Date of Birth_____
   Place of Birth_____
   Deceased_____ Interment_____
   Medical History_____

Number of Children_____

Name_____ Spouse_____
   Address_____ City_____ State_____ Zip_____
   Phone_____ Cell_____ Email_____
   Medical History_____
   Medication(s)_____

Name_____ Spouse_____
   Address_____ City_____ State_____ Zip_____
   Phone_____ Cell_____ Email_____
   Medical History_____
   Medication(s)_____

Name_____ Spouse_____
Address_____ City_____ State_____ Zip_____
Phone_____ Cell_____ Email_____
Medical History_____
Medication(s)_____

Number of Grandchildren_____
   Gender: Male_____ Female_____

Name_____ Spouse_____
   Address_____ City_____ State_____ Zip_____
   Medical History_____
   Medication(s)_____
   Parents Name_____

Name_____ Spouse_____
   Address_____ City_____ State_____ Zip_____

Phone_____ Cell_____ Email_____
Medical History_____
Medication(s)_____
Parents Name_____

Living Brothers & Sisters, Other Relatives_____
_____
_____
_____

Deceased Brothers & Sisters, Other Relatives_____
_____
_____
_____

Veterans Information:

Military Service: Branch of Service_____ Serial Number_____
               Name of War_____ Rank at discharge_____
               Date of: Induction_____
Discharge_____
               Location of Induction_____
               Location of Discharge_____
               Place of Service (Stationed)_____
_____

               Discharge from Service—Honorable _____
                              —Dishonorable_____
               Location of Discharge papers_____

ADDITIONAL INFORMATION FOR VETERANS:
To receive military funeral, you must include all the above information, including your discharge papers. Contact your funeral director for full details of eligibility.

CHAPTER 9

Insurance

INSURANCE...

There are countless forms of insurance available, from life insurance to property insurance and beyond. Your insurance needs may change frequently and should be updated and reviewed on a regular basis.

Health Insurance

When it comes to the estate planning process, it is particularly important to have health insurance information available. You should keep information regarding your insurance, including that carrier's contact information, readily available. This will come in handy when important decisions need to be made regarding your care, especially if you are incapacitated. Having health insurance information upfront can minimize the potential consequences encountered when making those decisions.

Property Insurance

Property insurance policies become especially valuable when an accident occurs causing physical or mental damage to the parties involved. Your policies specifically state how much money the insurance company will cover for property and medical costs as a result of the accident.

Applying for Insurance

When applying for insurance, you may need to include specific information to the insurance companies. The next few pages will recommend some of the information needed to apply for insurance. Also included is a sample list of the items needed to apply for Medicaid. This list is pertinent to Geauga County. The process may change depending on your county requirements.

LIFE INSURANCE...

Why is life insurance important?

1. It increases your estate, building wealth with a relatively small outlay of cash in the form of premiums.
2. It can provide financial assistance to loved ones upon your death.
3. It is received by beneficiaries free of income tax.
4. It may be owned by someone besides the insured and not be subject to death taxes.
5. It can be used to fund a business buy-out plan.
6. It could serve as a savings account (if it is whole life insurance).

Note: for further information on these benefits contact your Financial Advisor or Insurance Carrier and set up the correct type of insurance that will fit your needs.

Types of Policies

Most policies can be divided into two categories. Be sure to check with a financial or insurance advisor to choose the one that works best for you!

1. Term Policy—This has one common feature: There is no cash value built up from your premiums and you cannot borrow against this policy. This is a "simple life insurance" policy, offering the most coverage for the least cost. You have the ability to select the amount you want pay as an annual premium. If you die during the time you own the policy, your beneficiaries receive the insurance benefit.
2. Cash Value Policy—These are sometimes referred to as "whole life insurance" policies. Most of these policies have a savings account feature with varying investment returns.

There are several cash value policies: Whole (ordinary), universal, vanishing premium, joint first-to-die or second-to-die, and more.

PERSONAL HEALTH INSURANCE DOCUMENTS...

These are a few of the types of documents you'll need for the various types of insurance policies.

1. Life Insurance Policies (see the Personal Records tab)
   There is a worksheet to help you in gathering your materials.
2. Health Insurance Cards, Benefits, and Policy Descriptions
   There is a worksheet to help you in gathering your materials.
3. Medicare

Medicare is a national program that guarantees access to health insurance for Americans 65 and older and younger people with disabilities. Most people qualify for free hospital insurance when they turn 65 and start receiving Social Security benefits. Inpatient hospital care is covered under Part A of Medicare. This also includes home healthcare and Hospice care. Part B of Medicare covers outpatient medical services like doctor visits, outpatient hospital and ambulance services, and other medical services and supplies.

Unfortunately Medicare doesn't cover all health services. Dentures and routine dental care, eyeglasses, hearing aids, prescription drugs, and routine physical checkups are among the services not covered.

There are many rules associated with Medicare enrollment. You can contact your
Social Security Office for further details or call 1-800-MEDICARE.

Medicare Part C

This is another option for healthcare coverage that takes the place of Medicare parts A and B. Part C is a managed care option that provides you all the services covered by parts A and B plus a limited pharmacy benefit. Medicare Part C may not be offered as an option in Geauga County. There are several insurance companies that will offer Part C, utilizing networks of physicians and hospitals that must be used.

Part C is a good option for many people. When you enroll in one of these plans, there are not additional costs to your normal monthly payment to Medicare Part B. Part C can be canceled anytime.
Medigap or Medicare Supplement Insurance

These are insurance policies written specifically to pay for what Medicare will not. They are sold by private insurance companies but are highly regulated. You pay a premium to the insurance company and in return it will pay those medical expenses. To be eligible for Medigap, you must first be enrolled in parts A and B of Medicare.

If you would like more information about Medicare Supplement Insurance call the Ohio Department of Insurance 1-800-686-1578, and ask for their bulletin "Ohio Shopper's Guide to Medicare Supplement Insurance."

LONG TERM CARE INSURANCE . . .

Long Term Care (LTC) is a private insurance designed to help pay the high cost of long term care for an extended period due to illness and disability. Here are some basic factors to consider when you're thinking about long term care:

- Do you receive Medicaid or Supplemental Security Income? If so, LTC insurance is not needed.
- Do you have relatives or friends willing and able to take care of you? If you don't, LTC insurance could come in handy.
- Do you have enough saved income to pay for your long-term care? Remember you will have other expenses to take into consideration as well. If you do, you may not need LTC insurance.
- Would you be able to afford the insurance premiums of LTC insurance? Be sure to check with the insurance companies as to the costs. You may not be able to afford the cost of long term insurance.
- Will you qualify for LTC insurance? If you have a medical history or recent illness, you may have trouble getting a policy.

If you are unsure on LTC insurance, more information on LTC insurance is available within the new Ohio Shopper's Guide To Long Term Care Insurance. It is available free from the Ohio Department of Insurance. Call 1-800-686-1526.

LONG TERM DISABILITY INSURANCE

Long Term Disability (LTD) insurance allows you to receive a percentage of your earnings if you become ill or disabled and unable to work. The policy expires once you reach 65 years old.

YOUR LIFE INSURANCE POLICY RECORD

DATE _____

OWNER'S NAME_____

Address_____
City_____ State_____ Zip_____
Telephone_____ Cell_____ Zip_____ Fax_____
Email_____
Policy Number_____ Type_____

INSURANCE COMPANY NAME_____

Address_____
City_____ State_____ Zip_____
Telephone_____ Cell_____ Zip_____ Fax_____
Email_____
Policy Number_____ Policy Amount_____
Cash Value_____ Survivor Benefit_____
Premium_____ Date Due_____

First Beneficiary Name_____
Address_____ City_____
State_____ Zip_____
Phone_____ Cell_____ Fax_____
Email_____

Alternate Beneficiary Name_____
Address_____ City_____
State_____ Zip_____
Phone_____ Cell_____ Fax_____
Email_____

Alternate Beneficiary Name_____
Address_____ City_____
State_____ Zip_____
Phone_____ Cell_____ Fax_____
Email_____

HEALTH INSURANCE & MEDICATION

A. *HEALTH INSURANCE COMPANIES*

Primary Insurance Company Name_____
    Address_____
    City_____ State_____ Zip_____
    Phone_____ Fax_____ Email_____
Member Identification Number_____
Claims Office_____
Representative's Name_____
    Address_____
    City_____ State_____ Zip_____
    Phone_____ Fax_____ Email_____

Secondary Insurance Company Name_____
    Address_____
    City_____ State_____ Zip_____
    Phone_____ Fax_____ Email_____
Member Identification Number_____
Claims Office_____
Representative's Name_____
    Address_____
    City_____ State_____ Zip_____
    Phone_____ Fax_____ Email_____

B. *MEDICAL SUPPLIES*

Company Name_____
    Address_____
    City_____ State_____ Zip_____
    Phone_____ Fax_____ Email_____
Prescription Number_____ Name_____
Quantity_____ Milligrams_____
Physician Prescribed_____

C. *PHARMACY*

Pharmacy Name_____
   Address_____
     City_____ State_____ Zip_____
     Telephone_____ Fax_____ Email_____
Prescriptions_____
_____
_____

D. *MAIL AWAY PRESCRIPTIONS*

Company Name_____
   Address_____
     City_____ State_____ Zip_____
     Telephone_____ Fax_____ Email_____
Member Identification Number_____
Prescriptions_____
_____
_____

CHAPTER 10

Home Ownership

HOME OWNERSHIP DOCUMENTATION...

Home ownership is one of the largest and most important investments we make, and it is generally the most costly. Steps should be taken to insure your home is protected in the event of tragedy.

Depending on your circumstances, there are different types of home ownership. In this section we will briefly look at the different types of ownership and some of the steps that should be taken to protect your most valuable asset.

Keep in mind the means you choose to protect your assets can and do change over time. What may be practical now will change as you grow older. Therefore whenever you make a major decision or experience a life-changing event you should review your estate planning and make adjustments accordingly.

THE DIFFERENT HOME OWNERSHIP DOCUMENTS...

When we purchase a home or property we receive a deed. This gives us ownership to that particular parcel of property. Listed below are the different types of deeds.

Fee Simple

A Fee Simple deed means the life tenant has all rights of ownership during one's lifetime, along with the right to will it to anyone (except for dower rights). There are no inherent instructions in the deed as to who should receive the property upon the owner's death.

Life Estate

A Life Estate deed means the life tenant has the right to use and benefit from the property only during his or her lifetime. The life tenant does not have the right to will the property anyone. The person receiving the property upon the death of the life tenant was determined when the life estate was created.

Real Property (Tenancy in Common)

This type of ownership is in the form of co-ownership of real property comparable to a fee simple for single ownership. Each tenant owns an undivided share (not necessarily an equal share) of the property and has the right to dispose of that share without consent of the other (except for dower rights). Each undivided share is generally administered by Probate (or another instrument such as a trust) because as with a Fee Simple deed, there are no inherent instructions to decide who should receive the property upon the owner's death. This form of joint property ownership has an advantage: Either spouse can transfer property upon their death directly to children or through a trust to children rather than to the surviving spouse. This can result in estate settlement cost savings.

Joint Tenancy with Right of Survivorship (JTRS)

Joint Tenancy, also known as Joint Tenure, is a way of jointly holding property in such a way that there is no defined individual ownership. Additionally, the property automatically passes to the surviving owner at the death of the first owner. The survivor becomes the sole owner of the entire property. This transfer is not subject to Probate administration and implementation of the will. JTRS sidesteps the probate process and averts costs directly associated with probate, but tax forms still need to be filed for JTRS property as well as attorney fees associated with JTSR property transfers.

Tenancy By the Entirety

No more of this type of deed can be created in Ohio. However Tenancy By the Entirety deeds in existence prior to the change in the law in 1984 are still valid. This form of deed can only be created between a husband and wife and is similar to a JTRS deed in that they both carry the right of survivorship. This deed differs in that the debt of one spouse does not attach to the property. A Tenancy By the Entirety cannot be broken unless both spouses join in a deed to convey what they both own.

DOCUMENTS YOU MAY NEED BASED ON YOUR PARTICULAR CIRCUMSTANCES

Co-Ownership Property Agreement
Copy of Survey
Copy of Title Insurance Policy
Rental Agreement of Home or Apartment

INSURANCE

Homeowner's Insurance Policy
Fire Insurance Policy
Renter's Insurance
Appraisals and Evaluations of Valuable Personal Items
Copy of Property Tax Bill and Receipts

Are you Ready to Put Your Life in Order?

HOUSEHOLD INVENTORY

First Floor:

    Bedrooms _____ Bathrooms _____ Living Room _____
    Dining Room _____ Foyer _____ Kitchen _____
    Breakfast Room _____ Family Room _____
    Additional Room(s) _____

Second Floor:

    Bedrooms _____ Bathrooms _____ Living Room _____
    Dining Room _____ Foyer _____ Kitchen _____
    Breakfast Room _____ Family Room _____
    Additional Room(s) _____

Third Floor:

    Bedrooms _____ Bathrooms _____ Living Room _____
    Dining Room _____ Foyer _____ Kitchen _____
    Breakfast Room _____ Family Room _____
    Additional Room(s) _____

Appliances:

    Refrigerator _____ Dishwasher _____ Microwave _____
    Range Hood _____ Ice Maker _____ Wine Cooler _____
    Washer/Dryer_____ Others_____
    _____

For best inventory, take pictures of all assets and appliances.

SOCIAL SECURITY DOCUMENTS . . .

Photo copies of front and back of yours and spouses Social Security Card.

Your annual Social Security Statement.

Photocopies of the children's Social Security Cards.

Copies of checks or paid self-insurance taxes.

RETIREMENT

1. Pension plan, summary, description, type, annual statement, and annual individual pension benefit statement.

2. Is the Pension Plan in a lump sum or Payments?

3. Individual Retirement Accounts: IRA, Roth IRA, 401K, etc.

Participant's Name_____

Account No._____

Type of Plan_____

Name and Address of Custodial
Institution_____

Value to Date_____

Name of Primary Beneficiary_____

Name of Contingent Beneficiary_____

4. Joint and Survivor Pension Benefits

5. Type of Retirement Withdrawals

REAL ESTATE

Check one:
Own_____ Lease_____ Rent_____
Real Estate_____
Type_____

Owner(s) _____
Address_____ City_____ State_____
Zip_____ Telephone_____ Cell_____
Fax_____ Email_____

Legal Description on Deed of Property_____
_____
_____

Location_____
Property Tax Identification Number_____
Township_____

Name of Treasurer Office_____
Address_____ City_____ State_____
Zip_____
Telephone_____ Cell_____ Fax_____ Email_____
_____

Tax Market Value_____ Assessed Value_____
Property Taxes_____
Due_____

Original Building Cost_____ Cost of Improvements_____

REAL ESTATE INSURANCE

Insurance Company Name_____
Address_____ City_____ State_____ Zip_____
Telephone_____ Cell_____ Fax_____ Email_____
Policy Type_____ Policy Number_____ Premium_____
Telephone Number Customer Service_____ Claims_____
Service Specialist(s) Name_____ Extension_____

MORTGAGE

Institution Name_____
Address_____ City_____ State_____ Zip_____
Telephone_____ Cell_____ Fax_____ Email_____
Name(s) on Loan Account_____
Type of Loan_____ Account Number_____
Terms_____ Date Due_____
Cosigner(s)_____

Are you Ready to Put Your Life in Order?

NAMES & NUMBERS USED FOR HOME MAINTENANCE

Plumber_____ Phone _____

Electrician_____ Phone _____

Well Maintenance_____ Phone _____

Septic Maintenance_____ Phone _____

Location of Well & Septic tanks_____

_____

Handyman _____ Phone _____

Type of heating (circle): Oil Gas Propane Delivered

Company_____ Address_____

City_____ State_____ Phone_____

Account Number_____ Contact_____

Rubbish Removal_____ Phone_____

Others: Type_____ Name_____ Phone_____

_____

CHAPTER 11

Personal Property

PERSONAL PROPERTY...

As mentioned in the previous section, home ownership is perhaps the most important assets a person can have. In addition to home ownership, you may have accumulated many other forms of assets such as cash, cars, boats, household goods, and more.

In case of emergency it is important to have a documented list of your assets, where they're located, their current values, certificates and titles, and their locations. In this section we give you important worksheets to help organize all this information. Keep this as an original and make copies as necessary.

We have included **credit cards** in this section. These can be construed as an asset or a liability depending on whether they are paid off or left with an outstanding balance. In either case, keeping a list of all credit cards is particularly important. We suggest you make copies of all credit cards, front and back, and maintain these copies with the rest of your paperwork. We live in a society where credit card and personal identity theft is prevalent and keeping this information on file can be invaluable if ever you are faced with this scenario.

This section will give you and your loved ones important piece of mind when it comes time to deal with your personal property.

CREDIT CARD INFORMATION

Copy of Credit Card (Front and Back)

Bank Name _____
    Account Number _____
    Expiration Date _____
    Credit Line Available $_____
    Type of Card Visa: _____ MasterCard_____ Discover: _____
        Other: _____

Copy of Cancelled Credit Cards (Front and Back)

Bank Name _____
    Account Number _____
    Expiration Date _____
    Credit Line Available $_____
    Type of Card Visa: _____ MasterCard_____ Discover: _____
        Other: _____

It would also be prudent to keep copies of your most current statements.

CREDIT REPORTING AGENCIES...

It is extremely important that you receive an annual update of your credit report to protect yourself from unscrupulous fraud. Below is a list of the credit bureaus you may contact in order to receive these updated copies of your credit report.

Trans Union Corporation
Consumer Disclosure Center
P.O. Box 403
Springfield, PA 19064-0390
800-888-4213 (to order a copy of your credit report)
800-916-8800 (to ask questions about your credit report)
www.tuc.com

Equifax (formerly CBI/Equifax)
P.O. Box 740241
Atlanta, GA 30374-0341
800-685-1111
800-997-2493 (for residents of Colorado, Georgia, Maryland Massachusetts, New Jersey or Vermont)
www.equifax.com

Experian (formerly TRW Information System Inc.)
P.O. Box 403
Chester, PA 19022
888-EXPERIAN (888-397-3742)
www.experian.com

ASSETS

CASH ACCOUNTS Checking and Savings

Information needed for the following accounts:

Name of Institution_____
Branch & Address_____
Type of Account_____ Account Number_____
Name(s) on Account_____
Telephone_____ Fax_____ Email_____
Beneficiary(s)_____

Mutual Funds, Money Market Accounts, Credit Unions, Annuities

Custodial Institution_____
Branch & Address_____
Type of Fund_____ Account Number_____
Name(s) on Account_____
Telephone_____ Fax_____ Email_____
Beneficiary(s)_____
Certificate of Deposit

Name of Institution_____
Branch & Address_____
Account Number_____ Term_____ Expiration_____
Name(s) on Account_____
Beneficiary(s)_____

Individual Retirement Accounts (IRA's) or Pension Plan

Participant's Name_____
Account Number_____ (Mark): IRA or Pension_____
Name of Institution_____
Address of Institution_____
Telephone_____ Fax_____ Email_____
Primary Beneficiary_____
Contingent Beneficiary_____

SECURITY ACCOUNTS

For these accounts you may fill in the information or attach a copy of a recently monthly statement that carries the necessary information.

Name of Brokerage_____
Brokerage Address_____
Telephone_____ Cell_____ Fax_____ Email_____
Name(s) on Account_____
Account Number_____
Your Account Representative_____

Name of Brokerage_____
Brokerage Address_____
Telephone_____ Cell_____ Fax_____ Email_____
Name(s) on Account_____
Account Number_____
Your Account Representative_____

Name of Brokerage_____
Brokerage Address_____
Telephone_____ Cell_____ Fax_____ Email_____
Name(s) on Account_____
Account Number_____
Your Account Representative_____

Name of Brokerage_____
Brokerage Address_____
Telephone_____ Cell_____ Fax_____ Email_____
Name(s) on Account_____
Account Number_____
Your Account Representative_____

MUTUAL FUNDS, MONEY MARKET ACCOUNTS, CREDIT UNION STOCKS & BONDS

For these accounts you may fill in the information below or attach your monthly statement that contain all of the data.

(1) Institution Name_____

Address_____
Telephone_____ Fax_____ Email_____
Name(s) on the Account_____
Type of Account_____
Account Number_____ Amount_____

Beneficiaries_____

(2) Institution Name_____

Address_____
Telephone_____ Fax_____ Email_____
Name(s) on the Account_____
Type of Account_____
Account Number_____ Amount_____

Beneficiaries_____

(3) Firm Name_____

Broker_____

Address_____
Telephone_____ Fax_____ Email_____
Name(s) on Account_____
Type of Account_____ Amount_____
Beneficiaries_____ Financial Advisor_____
Portfolio_____

Automobile(s)

Make_____ Model_____ Year_____
Identification Number_____ Title Number_____
Owner(s) Name_____
    Address_____ City_____ State_____
    Zip_____ Telephone_____ Cell_____
    Fax_____ Email_____

Purchase Price_____ Date Purchased_____ Mileage_____
Location of Vehicle_____

Make_____ Model_____ Year_____
Identification Number_____ Title Number_____
Owner(s) Name_____
    Address_____ City_____ State_____
    Zip_____ Telephone_____ Cell_____
    Fax_____ Email_____

Purchase Price_____ Date Purchased_____ Mileage_____
Location of Vehicle_____

Make_____ Model_____ Year_____
Identification Number_____ Title Number_____
Owner(s) Name_____
    Address_____ City_____ State_____
    Zip_____ Telephone_____ Cell_____
    Fax_____ Email_____

Purchase Price_____ Date Purchased_____ Mileage_____
Location of Vehicle_____

Automobile Insurance Company_____
    Address_____ City_____ State_____ Zip_____
    Telephone_____ Cell_____ Fax_____
    Email_____

Policy Number_____ Premium Amount_____
Date Due_____ Expiration Date_____
Representative_____

Loan/Leasing Company_____
   Address_____ City_____ State_____ Zip_____
   Telephone_____ Cell_____ Fax_____
   Email_____
   Type_____ Amount_____
   Terms_____
   Account Number_____ Due Date_____

Boat(s)

Make_____ Model_____ Year_____
Identification Number_____ Title Number_____
Owner(s)_____
   Address_____ City_____ State_____ Zip_____
   Telephone_____ Cell_____ Fax_____
   Email_____
   Purchase Price_____ Date Purchased_____ Odometer____

Boat Insurance

Company Name_____
Address_____ City_____ State_____ Zip_____
Policy Number_____ Premium Amount_____
Due Date_____ Expiration Date_____
Representative_____

Loan Institution

Name_____
Address_____ City_____ State_____ Zip_____
Telephone_____ Fax_____ Email_____

Are you Ready to Put Your Life in Order?

Name(s) on Loan Account_____
Type of Loan_____ Account Number_____
Terms_____ Due Date_____
Cosigner(s)_____

Consider including important information like the location of keys for all above vehicles or combinations of locks if there are any.

CHAPTER 12

Household Income

HOUSEHOLD INCOME SOURCES

These worksheets serve to identify the sources of you and your family's income.

Source of Income	Monthly	Yearly
Employment		
Employee Stock Option Plan (ESOP)		
Pension/ Railroad Retirement		
Social Security Benefits		
Disability Benefits		
Disability Dependent Benefits		
Disability Retirement Benefits		
Disability Survivor Benefits		
Supplemental Security Income		
Veteran's Benefits		
Annuity Income		
IRA's. Keohs, 401K Plan		
Trust Income		
Interest/Dividend Income		
Rental Property Income		
Other Form of Income		

RETIREMENT ACCOUNTS (IRAS) OR PENSION PLANS

Participant's Name_____
Account Name_____ Account Number_____
Name of Custodial Institution_____
Address of Custodial Institution_____
Telephone_____ Cell_____ Fax_____ Email_____
Name of Primary Beneficiary_____
Name of Contingent Beneficiary_____

Participant's Name_____
Account Name_____ Account Number_____
Name of Custodial Institution_____
Address of Custodial Institution_____
Telephone_____ Cell_____ Fax_____ Email_____
Name of Primary Beneficiary_____
Name of Contingent Beneficiary_____

Participant's Name_____
Account Name_____ Account Number_____
Name of Custodial Institution_____
Address of Custodial Institution_____
Telephone_____ Cell_____ Fax_____ Email_____
Name of Primary Beneficiary_____
Name of Contingent Beneficiary_____

Participant's Name_____
Account Name_____ Account Number_____
Name of Custodial Institution_____
Address of Custodial Institution_____
Telephone_____ Cell_____ Fax_____ Email_____
Name of Primary Beneficiary_____
Name of Contingent Beneficiary_____

Are you Ready to Put Your Life in Order?

HOUSEHOLD INCOME, EMPLOYER & RETIREMENT

Name of Employee_____
   Address_____ City_____ State____ Zip____
   Telephone_____ Cell_____ Fax_____ Email_____
Employer Company_____
   Address_____ City_____ State____ Zip____
   Position_____ Income_____ Deductions_____
   Insurance Plan_____ Amount_____
   Insurance Company_____
   Insurance Address_____ City_____ State____ Zip____
   Beneficiary(s)_____
Retirement Plan_____ Amount_____
   Type of Retirement Plan_____
   Institution held at_____
   Address_____ City_____ State____ Zip____
   Telephone_____ Cell_____ Fax_____ Email_____
   Account Number_____
   Beneficiary(s)_____

Name of Employee_____
   Address_____ City_____ State____ Zip____
   Telephone_____ Cell_____ Fax_____ Email_____
Employer Company_____
   Address_____ City_____ State____ Zip____
   Position_____ Income_____ Deductions_____
   Insurance Plan_____ Amount_____
   Insurance Company_____
   Insurance Address_____ City_____ State____ Zip____
   Beneficiary(s)_____
Retirement Plan_____ Amount_____
   Type of Retirement Plan_____
   Institution held at_____
   Address_____ City_____ State____ Zip____
   Telephone_____ Cell_____ Fax_____ Email_____
   Account Number_____
   Beneficiary(s)_____

PARTNERSHIPS, LIMITED LIABILITY COMPANIES, & JOINT VENTURES

Whether you are in a partnership, have limited liability in a company, or have a joint venture in which you own interest, the following information is important.

Name of Partnership_____
General Partners_____
Address_____
Phone _____Cell _____Fax _____Email_____
Name of Owner as it appears on Partnership Records_____
Type of Partner _____General Partner _____Limited Partner _____
LLC_____

Amount of Original Investment_____

Name of Partnership_____
General Partners_____
Address_____
Phone _____Cell _____Fax _____Email_____
Name of Owner as it appears on the Partnership Records_____
Type of Partner _____General Partner _____Limited Partner _____
LLC_____

Amount of Original Investment_____

Name of Partnership_____
General Partners_____
Address_____
Phone _____Cell _____Fax _____Email_____
Name of Owner as it appears on the Partnership Records_____
Type of Partner _____General Partner _____Limited Partner _____
LLC_____

Amount of Original Investment_____

HOUSEHOLD EXPENSES

EXPENSES	MONTHLY	YEARLY
Home Mortgage		
Home Insurance		
Maintenance & Repair		
Heating		
Telephone(s) & Cell Phone(s)		
Food		
Clothing		
Personal Life Insurance(s)		
Health Insurance(s)		
Medical Costs		
Medication(s)		
Taxes—Federal		
State		
City		
Automobile(s) Loan(s)		
Plates		
Insurance(s)		
Maintenance		
Recreational Vehicle(s) Loan		
Plates		
Insurance(s)		
Maintenance		
Boat(s) Loan		
Plates Boat(s)/ Trailer(s)		
Insurance(s)		
Maintenance		
Charge Accounts		
Credit Cards		
Publications (Papers, Magazines, etc.)		
Miscellaneous		
TOTALS		

EXPENSES—UTILITIES

Electric Company_____ Account Number_____
    Address_____ City_____ State_____ Zip_____
    Telephone Business Office_____ Power Outages_____
    Date Due_____ Method of Payment_____
                               (Automatic, Deduction, Check, etc.)

Heating Company_____ Type_____ Account Number_____
    Address_____ City_____ State_____ Zip_____
    Telephone Business Office_____ Customer Service_____
    Date Due_____ Method of Payment_____
                               (Automatic, Deduction, Check, etc.)

Telephone Company_____ Account Number_____
    Address_____ City_____ State_____ Zip_____
    Telephone Business Office_____ Billing Inquires_____
    Hours_____ Method of Payment_____ Date Due_____
                               (Automatic, Deduction, Check, etc.)

Cell Phone Company_____ Account Number_____
    Address_____ City_____ State_____ Zip_____
    Telephone Customer Service_____ Billing Inquires_____
    Hours_____ Method of Payment_____ Date Due_____
                               (Automatic, Deduction, Check, etc.)

Television Company(s)_____
Type_____ Account Number(s)_____
Address_____ City_____ State_____ Zip_____
Telephone Customer Service_____ Billing Inquires_____
Hours_____ Method of Payment_____ Date Due_____
                               (Automatic, Deduction, Check, etc)

LIABILITIES

Type of Liabilities_____

Amount of Note $_____

Date Debt Incurred_____ Maturity Date_____

Type of Collateral_____

Lender Name_____

Lender Address_____
_____

Lender Phone: _____ Fax_____

Lender Email_____

Terms of Contract_____
_____
_____

Note Attached Yes_____ No_____

TAX RECORD DOCUMENTS

The following documents should be maintained for tax reporting purposes.

_____ Tax Returns should be saved for the Past Three Years
_____ Home Improvements Records

_____ Medical Expenses

_____ Donations to Charities

_____ Investment Expenses

_____ Employee Business Travel and Entertainment Expenses

_____ Higher Education Expenses

_____ Student Loan Interest Payments

_____ Real Estate Taxes, Mortgage Interest, Closing Costs

CHAPTER 13

Benefits Available for Veterans

BENEFITS AVAILABLE FOR VETERANS...

The Department of Veterans Affairs (VA)

Federal Benefits for Veterans and Dependents contain detailed information for benefits available for Veterans and their Dependents. The book covers the following:

1. VA Health Care
2. Veterans with Service Connected Disabilities
3. VA Pensions
4. Education & Training
5. Home Loan Guaranty
6. Burial and Memorial Benefits
7. Reserve & National Guard
8. Special Groups
9. Transition Assistance
10. Benefits for Dependents & Survivors
11. Appeals of VA Claims Decision
12. Military Medals and Records
13. Benefits Provided by Other Federal Agencies

Basic eligibility for VA healthcare benefits is based upon discharge from active military service, excluding dishonorable conditions. Active service refers to full-time service as a member of the Army, Navy, Air Force, Marine Corps, Coast Guard, or a commissioned officer of the Public Health Service. After financial assessments, veterans may qualify for medical services and supplies.

Veterans participating in the VA health registry can receive free medical examinations, including laboratory or other diagnostic tests deemed necessary by an examining clinician.

Veterans can receive prosthetic and sensory aids like artificial limbs, exclusive medical services, orthopedic braces, therapeutic shoes, wheelchairs, crutches, canes, walkers, and other durable medical equipment and supplies. VA healthcare will also provide hearing aids and eyeglasses. Special care medical services are available like inpatient care, extended care, medication, and outpatient care.

Copays apply to prescriptions and over the counter medication if receive from VA pharmacy. Certain veterans may be reimbursed for travel cost if they meet eligibility requirements.

INSURANCE

Life Insurance is available for veterans. Call 1-800-669-8477 Specialists are available between the hours of 8:30AM—6PM Eastern time, or visit the VA website at *http://www.insurance.va.gov* to discuss policies, premium payments, insurance dividends, address changes, policy loans, naming beneficiaries and reporting the death of the insured.

BENEFITS FOR DEPENDENTS & SURVIVORS

The Veterans Administration offers many benefits for dependents and survivors meeting eligibility. Terms of eligibility include: spouses cannot have remarried and children must be under age 18 (or under age 23 if attending a VA-approved school). Or the dependent must have become permanently incapable of self-support because of disability prior to the age of 18.

The following is a partial list of some of the benefits available to veterans: Bereavement Counseling, Death Pension, Dependency and Indemnity Compensation, Educational Assistance, Payments to Surviving Spouses, and VA Medical Care. Check the Federal Benefits for Veterans and Dependents for more benefits and greater detailed descriptions.

BURIAL & MEMORIAL BENEFITS

A veteran can be in a national cemetery for veterans, spouses, and dependents at no cost to the family. This includes the gravesite, grave-liner, opening and closing of the grave, headstone or marker, and perpetual care. A burial flag is also included.

The funeral director or next of kin makes interment arrangements by contacting the national cemetery in which burial is desired. Keep in mind the VA normally doesn't conduct funerals on weekends. Also, gravesites cannot be reserved, however the VA will honor reservations made under previous programs.

Remember, for reimbursement of burial expenses, burial allowances, plot allowances, and more, check with your funeral director for which benefits you may qualify.

REACHING VETERANS ADMINISTRATION CENTERS...

There is a complete list of all the clinics and community-based outpatient clinics for veterans in VA newsletters. Keep these newsletters handy.

For more information you can call a tele-nurse at 1-888-838-6446 OR visit the VA online at www.va.gov/visn10/

These are a few popular VAMC clinics:

Chillicothe VAMC
17273 State Route 104
Chillicothe, OH 45601
740-773-1141

Cincinnati VAMC
3200 Vine Street
Cincinnati, OH 45220
513-861-3100

Louis Stokes Wade Park VAMC
10701 East Boulevard
Cleveland, OH 44106
216-791-3800

Chalmers P. Wylie Outpatient Clinic
543 Taylor Avenue
Columbus, OH 43203
614-257-5200

Dayton VAMC
4100 West Third Street
Dayton, OH 45428
937-268-6511

The following are community-based outpatient clinics of the Veterans Administration:

Ohio: Athens 740-593-7314, Cambridge 740-432-1963, Lancaster 740-653-6145, Marietta 740-568-0412, Portsmouth 740-353-3236, Clermont County 513-943-3680 Brecksville VA Medical Center 440-526-3030, Akron 330-724-7715, Canton 330-489-4600, East Liverpool 330-386-4303, Lorain 440-244-3833, Mansfield 419-529-4602, McCafferty 216-939-0699, New Philadelphia 330-602-5339, Painesville 440-357-6740, Ravenna 330-296-3641, Sandusky 419-625-7350,

Warren 330-392-0311, Youngstown 330-740-9200, Grove City 614-257-5800, Marion 740-223-8089, Newark 740-788-8329, Zanesville 740-453-7725, Lima 419-222-5788, Middletown 513-423-8387, Springfield 937-328-3385

Kentucky—Ft. Thomas VA Campus 859-572-6202, Bellevue 859-392-3840, Florence 859-282-4480

Indiana—Dearborn, IN 812-539-2313, Richmond 765-973-6915

Chapter 14

Medical Decisions

PLANNING FOR MEDICAL DECISION-MAKING...

Advances in medicine and medical care have made it possible to survive illnesses or injuries that were once commonly fatal. In some cases the only method to keep a sick person alive is through life support systems. We call this "quantity of life," not "quality of life." Once such care has begun and there is no hope of recovery, who will make the decision to put an end to life support and allow the patient to die?

This decision often rests on the shoulders of the patient's family members after consulting with doctors. Because of questions legal liability and the changing relationship between doctors, patients, and families, these informal consultations are becoming less and less prevalent. These days the courts are often asked to appoint a guardian to make the healthcare decisions of an incapacitated person. This could be expensive, time consuming and often judgments may not reflect the personal wishes of the patient.

This doesn't have to be the case. There are legal tools available to make and enforce our personal wishes if we become disabled.

The following forms will give you the opportunity to express your wishes when it come to your personal affairs and the medical decisions you'd like made should you become disabled. You have several choices you can make now to assure your preferences are honored.

Durable Healthcare Power of Attorney or Health Care Proxy

A durable healthcare power of attorney or health care proxy allows you to select an agent (along with an alternate agent) to make the decisions in your best interest. These documents are now recognized everywhere in the United States, and give the agent legal authority to grant or refuse your own healthcare treatment. This can be expressed in both specific and general detail, as well as revoked or amended at any time. Your agent will be able to review your medical records, consult with your doctors and caregivers, and sign any forms needed to ensure the care you receive is according to your preferences.

Living Will or Health Care Declaration

Creating a living will or health care declaration allows you to express your preferences about your medical care in the event of a terminal illness. It lets you describe the extent to which you'd like to receive care when death is imminent. In other words, you can carry out your own personal wishes.

There is a difference between a healthcare power of attorney and a living will. A healthcare power of attorney gives the decision-making ability to an agent you selected along with a doctor's recommendation. A living will, on the other hand, applies only in the case of a terminal illness and becomes effective only when you are unable to express your own wishes.

Most people will sign both a durable healthcare power of attorney and a living will. You should read each of these documents carefully and be certain they are expressing your actual wishes. There are many pre-printed forms available, but these forms are often general in nature and may not meet your personal needs. Accordingly it would be best to consult an attorney or estate planner to counsel you as to your personal needs. These legal entities may be more critical in personalizing the documents necessary to carrying out your wishes.

HEALTHCARE POWER OF ATTORNEY & DIRECTIVES...

A. LIVING WILL
   a. Provides direction as to the medical care the person wishes to receive in the event of a terminal condition or being incapacitated
      i. This directive gives you the choice to choose whether or not you want your life prolonged despite terminal illness or vegetated state

B. POWER OF ATTORNEY
   a. Permits a designated person to make healthcare decisions in the event you are unable to speak for yourself

C. Do Not Resuscitate (DNR)
   a. Important points to remember when faced with a DNR situation
      i. Take into consideration the person's personal interests
      ii. Be sure to discuss all pros and cons with the physician

MEDICAL INFORMATION IS IN THE CARDS...

By John Arthur Hutchison

We spend time and money to draft living wills or healthcare powers of attorney, but what would happen if you suffered a medical emergency such as a heart attack or stroke, or you were involved in an automobile accident or any other type of accident that left you incapacitated? You do not carry the documents with you spelling out your wishes immediately to those who want to help you as to what you would have done.

There was an article in the *News Herald* stating the Lake County Recorder's Office was issuing cards that will notify emergency medical personnel where to find a patient's vital health documents. "Living Will," "Healthcare Power of Attorney" and "Do Not Resuscitate" wallet cards were made available, per the Lake County Recorder Frank A. Suponcic. The red-and-white laminated medical alert cards would inform emergency medical service personnel, emergency room physicians and hospital staff of the patient's medical forms that are on file in the recorder's office.

Many people have these documents prepared, but few can readily locate them, especially in the stressful times of medical emergencies. The medical alert card could be a bridge between an unresponsive patient and their medical wishes, especially for the elderly and those living alone. Emergency personnel such as paramedics and EMT's know to look for these types of items.

"When they're on scene to perform these lifesaving procedures they ask and they look for some type of living will, healthcare power of attorney or DNR order. This prevents conflict with the patients and the wishes of their families. A patient has rights, and emergency personnel like paramedics, EMT's, and physicians at the scene must respect these rights. If medical personnel are unsure whether a patient has a DNR order, they veer to the side of caution.

If documents for living wills, powers of attorney and DNR orders are already on file with the county recorder, there is no charge for the medical alert card, according to Suponcic. If the documents are not on file, there is a $28 per document fee as mandated by the Ohio Revised Code.

For more information, call the county recorder's office at (440) 350-2510.

ADDITIONAL FORMS . . .

Pages 110-121—State of Ohio—Health Care Power of Attorney forms:

This form of power of attorney is effective when you're not able to make healthcare decisions for yourself. You appoint an agent or attorney-in-fact to make these decisions. The document is witnessed or notarized to acknowledge your wishes.

Pages 122-127—State of Ohio—Living Will Declaration forms:

The living will declaration declares your wishes in regards to life-sustaining treatment when you are terminally ill or in a permanently unconscious state. This declaration honors your family and physician to express your legal right to refuse healthcare. This document is witnessed or notarized to acknowledge your wishes.

Pages 128-129—Donor Registry Enrollment form (Optional)

Page 130—Do Not Resuscitate (DNR) & (DNR-CC) orders

Keep in mind . . .

These are printed forms that may also be obtained from a healthcare facility, attorney, or your estate planner.

State of Ohio
Health Care Power of Attorney
of

_____
(Print Full Name)

_____
(Birth Date)

I state that this is my Health Care Power of Attorney and I revoke any prior Health Care Power of Attorney signed by me. I understand the nature and purpose of this document. If any provision is found to be invalid or unenforceable, it will not affect the rest of this document.

This Health Care Power of Attorney is in effect only when I cannot make health care decisions for myself. However, this does not require or imply that a court must declare me incompetent.

Definitions. Several legal and medical terms are used in this document. For convenience they are explained below.

Agent or **attorney-in-fact** means the adult I name in this Health Care Power of Attorney to make health care decisions for me.

Anatomical gift means a donation of all or part of a human body to take effect upon or after death.

Artificially or technologically supplied nutrition or hydration means the providing of food and fluids through intravenous or tube "feedings."

Cardiopulmonary resuscitation or **CPR** means treatment to try to restart breathing or heartbeat. CPR may be done by breathing into the mouth, pushing on the chest, putting a tube through the mouth or nose into the throat, administering medication, giving electric shock to the chest, or by other means.

Comfort care means any measure taken to diminish pain or discomfort, but not to postpone death.

Donor Registry Enrollment Form means a form that has been designed to allow individuals to specifically register their wishes regarding organ, tissue and eye donation with the Ohio Bureau of Motor Vehicles Donor Registry.

Do Not Resuscitate or **DNR Order** means a medical order given by my physician and written in my medical records that cardiopulmonary resuscitation or CPR is not to be administered to me.

Health care means any medical (including dental, nursing, psychological, and surgical) procedure, treatment, intervention or other measure used to maintain, diagnose or treat any physical or mental condition.

Health Care Power of Attorney means this document that allows me to name an adult person to act as my agent to make health care decisions for me if I become unable to do so.

Life-sustaining treatment means any health care, including artificially or technologically supplied nutrition and hydration, that will serve mainly to prolong the process of dying.

Living Will Declaration or **Living Will** means another document that lets me specify the health care I want to receive if I become terminally ill or permanently unconscious and cannot make my wishes known.

Permanently unconscious state means an irreversible condition in which I am permanently unaware of myself and surroundings. My physician and one other physician must examine me and agree that the total loss of higher brain function has left me unable to feel pain or suffering.

Principal means the person signing this document.

Terminal condition or **terminal illness** means an irreversible, incurable and untreatable condition caused by disease, illness or injury. My physician and one other physician will have examined me and believe that I cannot recover and that death is likely to occur within a relatively short time if I do not receive life-sustaining treatment.

[Instructions and other information to assist in completing this document are set forth within brackets and in italic type.]

Naming of My Agent. The person named below is my agent who will make health care decisions for me as authorized in this document.

Agent's Name: _____

Agent's Current Address: _____

Agent's Current Telephone Number: _____

Naming of Alternate Agents. *[Note: You do not need to name alternate agents. You also may name just one alternate agent. If you do not name alternate agents or name just one alternate agent, you may wish to cross out the unused lines.]*

Should my agent named above not be immediately available or be unwilling or unable to make decisions for me, then I name, in the following order of priority, the following persons as my alternate agents:

First Alternate Agent:	Second Alternate Agent:
Name: _____	Name: _____
Address: _____	Address: _____
_____	_____
Telephone: _____	Telephone: _____

Any person can rely on a statement by any alternate agent named above that he or she is properly acting under this document and such person does not have to make any further investigation or inquiry.

Guidance to Agent. My agent will make health care decisions for me based on the instructions that I give in this document and on my wishes otherwise known to my agent. If my agent believes that my wishes as made known to my agent conflict with what is in this document, this document will control. If my wishes are unclear or unknown, my agent will make health care decisions in my best interests. My agent will determine my best interests after considering the benefits, the burdens, and the risks that might result from a given decision. If no agent is available, this document will guide decisions about my health care.

Authority of Agent. My agent has full and complete authority to make all health care decisions for me whenever I cannot make such decisions, unless I have otherwise indicated below. This authority includes, but is not limited to, the following: *[Note: Cross out any authority that you do **not** want your agent to have.]*

1. To consent to the administration of pain-relieving drugs or treatment or procedures (including surgery) that my agent, upon medical advice, believes may provide comfort to me, even though such drugs, treatment or procedures may hasten my death. My comfort and freedom from pain are important to me and should be protected by my agent and physician.

2. If I am in a terminal condition, to give, to withdraw or to refuse to give informed consent to life-sustaining treatment, including artificially or technologically supplied nutrition or hydration.

3. To give, withdraw or refuse to give informed consent to any health care procedure, treatment, intervention or other measure.

4. To request, review, and receive any information, verbal or written, regarding my physical or mental health, including, but not limited to, all my medical and health care records.

5. To consent to further disclosure of information, and to disclose medical and related information concerning my condition and treatment to other persons.

6. To execute for me any releases or other documents that may be required in order to obtain medical and related information.

7. To execute consents, waivers, and releases of liability for me and for my estate to all persons who comply with my agent's instructions and decisions. To indemnify and hold harmless, at my expense, any third party who acts under this Health Care Power of Attorney. I will be bound by such indemnity entered into by my agent.

8. To select, employ, and discharge health care personnel and services providing home health care and the like.

9. To select, contract for my admission to, transfer me to, or authorize my discharge from any medical or health care facility, including, but not limited to, hospitals, nursing homes, assisted living facilities, hospices, adult homes and the like.

10. To transport me or arrange for my transportation to a place where this Health Care Power of Attorney is honored, should I become unable to make health care decisions for myself in a place where this document is not enforced.

11. To complete and sign for me the following:

    (a) Consents to health care treatment, or the issuance of Do Not Resuscitate (DNR) Orders or other similar orders; and

    (b) Requests for my transfer to another facility, to be discharged against health care advice, or other similar requests; and

    (c) Any other document desirable to implement health care decisions that my agent is authorized to make pursuant to this document.

Special Instructions. **By placing my initials at number 3 below, I want to specifically authorize my agent to refuse, or if treatment has commenced, to withdraw consent to, the provision of artificially or technologically supplied nutrition or hydration if:**

1. **I am in a permanently unconscious state; and**

2. **My physician and at least one other physician who has examined me have determined, to a reasonable degree of medical certainty, that artificially or technologically supplied nutrition and hydration will not provide comfort to me or relieve my pain; and**

3. **I have placed my initials on this line: _____**

Limitations of Agent's Authority. I understand that under Ohio law, there are five limitations to the authority of my agent:

1. My agent cannot order the withdrawal of life-sustaining treatment unless I am in a terminal condition or a permanently unconscious state, and two physicians have confirmed the diagnosis and have determined that I have no reasonable possibility of regaining the ability to make decisions; and

2. My agent cannot order the withdrawal of any treatment given to provide comfort care or to relieve pain; and

3. If I am pregnant, my agent cannot refuse or withdraw informed consent to health care if the refusal or withdrawal would end my pregnancy, unless the pregnancy or health care would create a substantial risk to my life or two physicians determine that the fetus would not be born alive; and

4. My agent cannot order the withdrawal of artificially or technologically supplied nutrition or hydration unless I am terminally ill or permanently unconscious and two physicians agree that nutrition or hydration will no longer provide comfort or relieve pain and, in the event that I am permanently unconscious, I have given a specific direction to withdraw nutrition or hydration elsewhere in this document; and

5. If I previously consented to any health care, my agent cannot withdraw that treatment unless my condition has significantly changed so that the health care is significantly less beneficial to me, or unless the health care is not achieving the purpose for which I chose the health care.

Additional Instructions or Limitations. I may give additional instructions or impose additional limitations on the authority of my agent. *[Note: On the lines below you may write in additional instructions or limitations. Here you may include any specific instructions or limitations you consider appropriate, such as instructions to refuse specific types of treatment that are inconsistent with your religious beliefs or unacceptable to you for any other reason. If the space below is not sufficient, you may attach additional pages. If you include additional instructions or limitations here and your wishes change, you should complete a new Health Care Power of Attorney and tell your agent about the changes. If you do not have any additional instructions or limitations, you may wish to write "None" below or cross out the unused lines.]*

No Expiration Date. This Health Care Power of Attorney will have no expiration date and will not be affected by my disability or by the passage of time.

Guardian. I intend that the authority given to my agent will eliminate the need for any court to appoint a guardian of my person. However, should such proceedings start, I nominate my agent to serve as the guardian of my person, without bond.

Enforcement by Agent. My agent may take for me, at my expense, any action my agent considers advisable to enforce my wishes under this document.

Release of Agent's Personal Liability. My agent will not incur any personal liability to me or my estate for making reasonable choices in good faith concerning my health care.

Copies the Same as Original. Any person may rely on a copy of this document.

Out of State Application. I intend that this document be honored in any jurisdiction to the extent allowed by law.

Living Will. I have completed a Living Will:_____ ☐ Yes _____ ☐ No

Anatomical Gift(s). I have made my wishes known regarding organ and tissue donation in my Living Will:_____ ☐ Yes _____ ☐ No

Donor Registry Enrollment Form. I have completed the Donor Registry Enrollment Form: _____ ☐ Yes _____ ☐ No

SIGNATURE
[See next page for witness or notary requirements.]

I understand the purpose and effect of this document and sign my name to this Health Care Power of Attorney on _____, 20 ____, at _____, Ohio.

_____
PRINCIPAL

[You are responsible for telling members of your family and your physician about this document and the name of your agent. You also may wish, but are not required to tell your religious advisor and your lawyer that you have signed a Health Care Power of Attorney. You may wish to give a copy to each person notified.]

[You may choose to file a copy of this Health Care Power of Attorney with your county recorder for safekeeping.]

WITNESSES OR NOTARY ACKNOWLEDGMENT
[Choose one.]

[This Health Care Power of Attorney will not be valid unless it either is signed by two eligible witnesses who are present when you sign or are present when you acknowledge your signature, or it is acknowledged before a Notary Public.]

*[The following persons **cannot** serve as a witness to this Health Care Power of Attorney: the agent; any successor agent named in this document; your spouse; your children; anyone else related to you by blood, marriage or adoption; your attending physician; or, if you are in a nursing home, the administrator of the nursing home.]*

Witnesses. I attest that the Principal signed or acknowledged this Health Care Power of Attorney in my presence, that the Principal appears to be of sound mind and not under or subject to duress, fraud or undue influence. I further attest that I am not an agent designated in this document, I am not the attending physician of the Principal, I am not the administrator of a nursing home in which the Principal is receiving care, and I am an adult not related to the Principal by blood, marriage or adoption.

_____ residing at _____
Signature

_____ _____, _____
Print Name

Dated: _____, 20_____

_____ residing at _____
Signature

_____ _____, _____
Print Name

Dated: _____, 20_____

OR

Notary Acknowledgment.
State of Ohio
County of _____ ss.

On _____, 20_____, before me, the undersigned Notary Public, personally appeared _____, known to me or satisfactorily proven to be the person whose name is subscribed to the above Health Care Power of Attorney as the Principal, and who has acknowledged that (s)he executed the same for the purposes expressed therein. I attest that the Principal appears to be of sound mind and not under or subject to duress, fraud or undue influence.

_____
Notary Public

My Commission Expires: _____

[This notice is included in this printed form as required by Ohio Revised Code § 1337.17.]

NOTICE TO ADULT EXECUTING THIS DOCUMENT

This is an important legal document. Before executing this document, you should know these facts:

This document gives the person you designate (the attorney in fact) the power to make MOST health care decisions for you if you lose the capacity to make informed health care decisions for yourself. This power is effective only when your attending physician determines that you have lost the capacity to make informed health care decisions for yourself and, notwithstanding this document, as long as you have the capacity to make informed health care decisions for yourself, you retain the right to make all medical and other health care decisions for yourself.

You may include specific limitations in this document on the authority of the attorney in fact to make health care decisions for you.

Subject to any specific limitations you include in this document, if your attending physician determines that you have lost the capacity to make an informed decision on a health care matter, the attorney in fact GENERALLY will be authorized by this document to make health care decisions for you to the same extent as you could make those decisions yourself, if you had the capacity to do so. The authority of the attorney in fact to make health care decisions for you GENERALLY will include the authority to give informed consent, to refuse to give informed consent, or to withdraw informed consent to any care, treatment, service, or procedure to maintain, diagnose, or treat a physical or mental condition.

HOWEVER, even if the attorney in fact has general authority to make health care decisions for you under this document, the attorney in fact NEVER will be authorized to do any of the following:

(1) Refuse or withdraw informed consent to life-sustaining treatment (unless your attending physician and one other physician who examines you determine, to a reasonable degree of medical certainty and in accordance with reasonable medical standards, that either of the following applies:

(a) You are suffering from an irreversible, incurable and untreatable condition caused by disease, illness, or injury from which (i) there can be no recovery and (ii) your death is likely to occur within a relatively short time if life-sustaining treatment is not administered, and your attending physician additionally determines, to a reasonable degree of medical certainty and in accordance with reasonable medical standards, that there is no reasonable possibility that you will regain the capacity to make informed health care decisions for yourself.

[This notice is included in this printed form as required by Ohio Revised Code § 1337.17.]

(b) You are in a state of permanent unconsciousness that is characterized by you being irreversibly unaware of yourself and your environment and by a total loss of cerebral cortical functioning, resulting in you having no capacity to experience pain or suffering, and your attending physician additionally determines, to a reasonable degree of medical certainty and in accordance with reasonable medical standards, that there is no reasonable possibility that you will regain the capacity to make informed health care decisions for yourself);

(2) Refuse or withdraw informed consent to health care necessary to provide you with comfort care (except that, if the attorney in fact is not prohibited from doing so under (4) below, the attorney in fact could refuse or withdraw informed consent to the provision of nutrition or hydration to you as described under (4) below). **(You should understand that comfort care is defined in Ohio law to mean artificially or technologically administered sustenance (nutrition) or fluids (hydration) when administered to diminish your pain or discomfort, not to postpone your death, and any other medical or nursing procedure, treatment, intervention, or other measure that would be taken to diminish your pain or discomfort, not to postpone your death. Consequently, if your attending physician were to determine that a previously described medical or nursing procedure, treatment, intervention, or other measure will not or no longer will serve to provide comfort to you or alleviate your pain, then, subject to (4) below, your attorney in fact would be authorized to refuse or withdraw informed consent to the procedure, treatment, intervention, or other measure.);**

(3) Refuse or withdraw informed consent to health care for you if you are pregnant and if the refusal or withdrawal would terminate the pregnancy (unless the pregnancy or health care would pose a substantial risk to your life, or unless your attending physician and at least one other physician who examines you determine, to a reasonable degree of medical certainty and in accordance with reasonable medical standards, that the fetus would not be born alive);

(4) **Refuse or withdraw informed consent to the provision of artificially or technologically administered sustenance (nutrition) or fluids (hydration) to you, unless:**

(a) **You are in a terminal condition or in a permanently unconscious state.**

[This notice is included in this printed form as required by Ohio Revised Code § 1337.17.]

(b) Your attending physician and at least one other physician who has examined you determine, to a reasonable degree of medical certainty and in accordance with reasonable medical standards, that nutrition or hydration will not or no longer will serve to provide comfort to you or alleviate your pain.

(c) If, but only if, you are in a permanently unconscious state, you authorize the attorney in fact to refuse or withdraw informed consent to the provision of nutrition or hydration to you by doing both of the following in this document:

(i) Including a statement in capital letters or other conspicuous type, including, but not limited to, a different font, bigger type, or boldface type, that the attorney in fact may refuse or withdraw informed consent to the provision of nutrition or hydration to you if you are in a permanently unconscious state and if the determination that nutrition or hydration will not or no longer will serve to provide comfort to you or alleviate your pain is made, or checking or otherwise marking a box or line (if any) that is adjacent to a similar statement on this document;

(ii) Placing your initials or signature underneath or adjacent to the statement, check, or other mark previously described.

(d) Your attending physician determines, in good faith, that you authorized the attorney in fact to refuse or withdraw informed consent to the provision of nutrition or hydration to you if you are in a permanently unconscious state by complying with the above requirements of (4)(c)(i) and (ii) above.

(5) Withdraw informed consent to any health care to which you previously consented, unless a change in your physical condition has significantly decreased the benefit of that health care to you, or unless the health care is not, or is no longer, significantly effective in achieving the purposes for which you consented to its use.

Additionally, when exercising authority to make health care decisions for you, the attorney in fact will have to act consistently with your desires or, if your desires are unknown, to act in your best interest. You may express your desires to the attorney in fact by including them in this document or by making them known to the attorney in fact in another manner.

When acting pursuant to this document, the attorney in fact GENERALLY will have the same rights that you have to receive information about proposed health care, to review health care records, and to consent to the disclosure of health care records. You can limit that right in this document if you so choose.

Are you Ready to Put Your Life in Order?

[This notice is included in this printed form as required by Ohio Revised Code § 1337.17.]

Generally, you may designate any competent adult as the attorney in fact under this document. However, you CANNOT designate your attending physician or the administrator of any nursing home in which you are receiving care as the attorney in fact under this document. Additionally, you CANNOT designate an employee or agent of your attending physician, or an employee or agent of a health care facility at which you are being treated, as the attorney in fact under this document, unless either type of employee or agent is a competent adult and related to you by blood, marriage, or adoption, or unless either type of employee or agent is a competent adult and you and the employee or agent are members of the same religious order.

This document has no expiration date under Ohio law, but you may choose to specify a date upon which your durable power of attorney for health care will expire. However, if you specify an expiration date and then lack the capacity to make informed health care decisions for yourself on that date, the document and the power it grants to your attorney in fact will continue in effect until you regain the capacity to make informed health care decisions for yourself.

You have the right to revoke the designation of the attorney in fact and the right to revoke this entire document at any time and in any manner. Any such revocation generally will be effective when you express your intention to make the revocation. However, if you made your attending physician aware of this document, any such revocation will be effective only when you communicate it to your attending physician, or when a witness to the revocation or other health care personnel to whom the revocation is communicated by such a witness communicates it to your attending physician.

If you execute this document and create a valid durable power of attorney for health care with it, it will revoke any prior, valid durable power of attorney for health care that you created, unless you indicate otherwise in this document.

This document is not valid as a durable power of attorney for health care unless it is acknowledged before a notary public or is signed by at least two adult witnesses who are present when you sign or acknowledge your signature. No person who is related to you by blood, marriage, or adoption may be a witness. The attorney in fact, your attending physician, and the administrator of any nursing home in which you are receiving care also are ineligible to be witnesses.

If there is anything in this document that you do not understand, you should ask your lawyer to explain it to you.

© *December 2004. May be reprinted and copied for use by the public, attorneys, medical and osteopathic physicians, hospitals, bar associations, medical societies, and nonprofit associations and organizations. It may not be reproduced commercially for sale at a profit.*

State of Ohio
Living Will Declaration
Notice to Declarant

The purpose of this Living Will Declaration is to document your wish that life-sustaining treatment, including artificially or technologically supplied nutrition and hydration, be withheld or withdrawn if you are unable to make informed medical decisions and are in a terminal condition or in a permanently unconscious state. This Living Will Declaration does not affect the responsibility of health care personnel to provide comfort care to you. Comfort care means any measure taken to diminish pain or discomfort, but not to postpone death.

If you would not choose to limit any or all forms of life-sustaining treatment, including CPR, you have the legal right to so choose and may wish to state your medical treatment preferences in writing in a different document.

Under Ohio law, a Living Will Declaration is applicable only to individuals in a terminal condition or a permanently unconscious state. If you wish to direct medical treatment in other circumstances, you should prepare a Health Care Power of Attorney. If you are in a terminal condition or a permanently unconscious state, this Living Will Declaration controls over a Health Care Power of Attorney.

You should consider completing a new Living Will Declaration if your medical condition changes, or if you later decide to complete a Health Care Power of Attorney. If you have both documents, you should keep copies of both documents together, with your other important papers, and bring copies of both your Living Will and your Health Care Power of Attorney with you whenever you are a patient in a health care facility.

Ohio Hospice & Palliative Care Organization | Ohio State Medical Association | Ohio Hospital Association | Ohio Osteopathic Association | OSBA Ohio State Bar Association

State of Ohio
Living Will Declaration
of

_____
(Print Full Name)

_____
(Birth Date)

I state that this is my Ohio Living Will Declaration. I am of sound mind and not under or subject to duress, fraud or undue influence. I am a competent adult who understands and accepts the consequences of this action. I voluntarily declare my wish that my dying not be artificially prolonged. If I am unable to give directions regarding the use of life-sustaining treatment when I am in a terminal condition or a permanently unconscious state, I intend that this Living Will Declaration be honored by my family and physicians as the final expression of my legal right to refuse health care.

Definitions. Several legal and medical terms are used in this document. For convenience they are explained below.

Anatomical gift means a donation of all or part of a human body to take effect upon or after death.

Artificially or technologically supplied nutrition or hydration means the providing of food and fluids through intravenous or tube "feedings."

Cardiopulmonary resuscitation or **CPR** means treatment to try to restart breathing or heartbeat. CPR may be done by breathing into the mouth, pushing on the chest, putting a tube through the mouth or nose into the throat, administering medication, giving electric shock to the chest, or by other means.

Declarant means the person signing this document.

Donor Registry Enrollment Form means a form that has been designed to allow individuals to specifically register their wishes regarding organ, tissue and eye donation with the Ohio Bureau of Motor Vehicles Donor Registry.

Do Not Resuscitate or **DNR Order** means a medical order given by my physician and written in my medical records that cardiopulmonary resuscitation or CPR is not to be administered to me.

Health care means any medical (including dental, nursing, psychological, and surgical) procedure, treatment, intervention or other measure used to maintain, diagnose or treat any physical or mental condition.

Health Care Power of Attorney means another document that allows me to name an adult person to act as my agent to make health care decisions for me if I become unable to do so.

Life-sustaining treatment means any health care, including artificially or technologically supplied nutrition and hydration, that will serve mainly to prolong the process of dying.

Living Will Declaration or **Living Will** means this document that lets me specify the health care I want to receive if I become terminally ill or permanently unconscious and cannot make my wishes known.

Permanently unconscious state means an irreversible condition in which I am permanently unaware of myself and my surroundings. My physician and one other physician must examine me and agree that the total loss of higher brain function has left me unable to feel pain or suffering.

Terminal condition or **terminal illness** means an irreversible, incurable and untreatable condition caused by disease, illness or injury. My physician and one other physician will have examined me and believe that I cannot recover and that death is likely to occur within a relatively short time if I do not receive life-sustaining treatment.

[Instructions and other information to assist in completing this document are set forth within brackets and in italic type.]

Health Care if I Am in a Terminal Condition. If I am in a terminal condition and unable to make my own health care decisions, I direct that my physician shall:

1. Administer no life-sustaining treatment, including CPR and artificially or technologically supplied nutrition or hydration; and
2. Withdraw such treatment, including CPR, if such treatment has started; and
3. Issue a DNR Order; and
4. Permit me to die naturally and take no action to postpone my death, providing me with only that care necessary to make me comfortable and to relieve my pain.

Health Care if I Am in a Permanently Unconscious State. If I am in a permanently unconscious state, I direct that my physician shall:

1. Administer no life-sustaining treatment, including CPR, except for the provision of artificially or technologically supplied nutrition or hydration unless, in the following paragraph, I have authorized its withholding or withdrawal; and
2. Withdraw such treatment, including CPR, if such treatment has started; and
3. Issue a DNR Order; and
4. Permit me to die naturally and take no action to postpone my death, providing me with only that care necessary to make me comfortable and to relieve my pain.

Special Instructions. By placing my initials at number 3 below, I want to specifically authorize my physician to withhold or to withdraw artificially or technologically supplied nutrition or hydration if:

1. I am in a permanently unconscious state; and
2. My physician and at least one other physician who has examined me have determined, to a reasonable degree of medical certainty, that artificially or technologically supplied nutrition and hydration will not provide comfort to me or relieve my pain; and
3. I have placed my initials on this line: _____

Notifications. *[Note: You do not need to name anyone. If no one is named, the law requires your attending physician to make a reasonable effort to notify one of the following persons in the order named: your guardian, your spouse, your adult children who are available, your parents, or a majority of your adult siblings who are available.]*

In the event my attending physician determines that life-sustaining treatment should be withheld or withdrawn, my physician shall make a reasonable effort to notify one of the persons named below, in the following order of priority:

[Note: If you do not name two contacts, you may wish to cross out the unused lines.]

First Contact:	Second Contact:
Name: _____	Name: _____
Address: _____	Address: _____
_____	_____
Telephone: _____	Telephone: _____

Anatomical Gift (optional)

INSTRUCTIONS: If you elect to make an anatomical gift, please complete and file the attached "Donor Registry Enrollment Form" with the Ohio Bureau of Motor Vehicles to ensure that your wishes will be honored.

[____] I wish to make an anatomical gift.

[____] I *do not* wish to make an anatomical gift.

Upon my death, the following are my directions regarding donation of all or part of my body:
In the hope that I, _____ (name of donor), may help others upon my death, I hereby give the following body parts: _____
(indicate specific parts or all body parts) for any purpose authorized by law: transplantation, therapy, research or education. *[Cross out any purpose that is unacceptable to you.]*

This is a legal document under the Uniform Anatomical Gift Act or similar laws.

If I do not indicate a desire to donate all or part of my body by filling in the lines above, no presumption is created about my desire to make or refuse to make an anatomical gift.

Donor Registry Enrollment Form. I have completed the Donor Registry Enrollment Form:

_____ ☐ Yes _____ ☐ No

> **NOTE**: If you modify or revoke your decision regarding anatomical gifts, please remember to make those changes in your Living Will, Health Care Power of Attorney, and Donor Registry Enrollment Form.

No Expiration Date. This Living Will Declaration will have no expiration date. However, I may revoke it at any time.

Copies the Same as Original. Any person may rely on a copy of this document.

Out of State Application. I intend that this document be honored in any jurisdiction to the extent allowed by law.

Health Care Power of Attorney. I have completed a Health Care Power of Attorney:

_____ ☐ Yes _____ ☐ No

SIGNATURE
[See below for witness or notary requirements.]

I understand the purpose and effect of this document and sign my name to this Living Will Declaration on _____, 20 _____, at _____, Ohio.

_____
DECLARANT

[You are responsible for telling members of your family, the agent named in your Health Care Power of Attorney (if you have one), and your physician about this document. You also may wish to tell your religious advisor and your lawyer that you have signed a Living Will Declaration. You may wish to give a copy to each person notified.]

[You may choose to file a copy of this Living Will Declaration with your county recorder for safekeeping.]

WITNESSES OR NOTARY ACKNOWLEDGMENT
[Choose one.]

[This Living Will Declaration will not be valid unless it either is signed by two eligible witnesses who are present when you sign or are present when you acknowledge your signature, or it is acknowledged before a Notary Public.]

*[The following persons **cannot** serve as a witness to this Living Will Declaration: the agent or*

Are you Ready to Put Your Life in Order?

any successor agent named in your Health Care Power of Attorney; your spouse; your children; anyone else related to you by blood, marriage or adoption; your attending physician; or, if you are in a nursing home, the administrator of the nursing home.]

Witnesses. I attest that the Declarant signed or acknowledged this Living Will Declaration in my presence, and that the Declarant appears to be of sound mind and not under or subject to duress, fraud or undue influence. I further attest that I am not an agent designated in the Declarant's Health Care Power of Attorney, I am not the attending physician of the Declarant, I am not the administrator of a nursing home in which the Declarant is receiving care, and I am an adult not related to the Declarant by blood, marriage or adoption.

_____ residing at _____
Signature

_____ _____, _____
Print Name

Dated: _____, 20_____

_____ residing at _____
Signature

_____ _____, _____
Print Name

Dated: _____, 20_____

OR

Notary Acknowledgment.
State of Ohio
County of _____ ss.

On _____, 20_____, before me, the undersigned Notary Public, personally appeared _____, known to me or satisfactorily proven to be the person whose name is subscribed to the above Living Will Declaration as the Declarant, and who has acknowledged that (s)he executed the same for the purposes expressed therein. I attest that the Declarant appears to be of sound mind and not under or subject to duress, fraud or undue influence.

_____
Notary Public

My Commission Expires: _____

© December 2004. *May be reprinted and copied for use by the public, attorneys, medical and osteopathic physicians, hospitals, bar associations, medical societies, and nonprofit associations and organizations. It may not be reproduced commercially for sale at a profit.*

DONOR REGISTRY ENROLLMENT FORM (OPTIONAL)

(name of donor)

INSTRUCTIONS: In addition to completing the references to Anatomical Gifts in your Living Will and Ohio Health Care Power of Attorney you should also complete and file the "Donor Registry Enrollment Form" with the Ohio Bureau of Motor Vehicles to ensure that your wishes concerning organ and tissue donation will be honored. This document will serve as your consent to recover the organ and/or tissues indicated at the time of your death, if medically possible. In completing this form, your wishes will be recorded in the Ohio Donor Registry and will be accessible only to the appropriate organ, tissue or eye recovery organizations. Be sure to share your wishes in this area with loved ones and friends so they are aware of your intentions.

To register for the Donor Registry, please complete this form, detach and send the original to:

Ohio Bureau of Motor Vehicles
ATTN: Record Clearance Unit
P.O. Box 16784
Columbus, Ohio 43216-6784

Make a copy of this form and retain it as part of your Living Will Declaration.

[This form must be signed by two witnesses. If the donor is under the age of 18, a parent or legal guardian must sign as one of the two witnesses.]

[This form should be used to state your intentions to be included in or removed from the Ohio Bureau of Motor Vehicles Donor Registry.]

Please indicate below:

☐ Please include me in the Donor Registry

☐ Please remove me from the Donor Registry

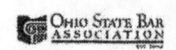

Are you Ready to Put Your Life in Order?

Print or type full name of living donor _____
Mailing Address _____
City _____ State _____ Zip _____
Phone ( ) _____ Date of Birth _____
Driver's License or ID Card Number _____
Social Security Number _____

In the hope that I, _____ (name of donor), may help others upon my death, the following are my directions regarding donation of all or part of my body.

☐ On my death, I make an anatomical gift of my organs, tissues, and eyes for any purpose authorized by law.

OR

☐ On my death, I make an anatomical gift of the following specified organ, tissues, or eyes for any purposes indicated below:

☑ Any or all   ☐ Liver   ☐ Bone/ligament   ☐ Heart valves
☐ Heart   ☐ Kidneys   ☐ Veins   ☐ Skin
☐ Lung   ☐ Pancreas   ☐ Eyes   ☐ Other

☑ Any purpose authorized by law or, specifically as indicated below:
    ☐ Transplantation
    ☐ Therapy
    ☐ Research
    ☐ Education
    ☐ Advancement of medical science
    ☐ Advancement of dental science

_____
Signature of Donor

_____   _____
Date of Birth of Donor   Date Signed

_____   _____
Witness   Date

_____   _____
Witness   Date

129

DO NOT RESUSCITATE (DNR) ORDER . . .

With your medical directives there are two more medical requests you may wish to add to your health care power of attorney and living will declaration. They are Do Not Resuscitate (DNR) and Do Not Resuscitate-Comfort Care (DNR-CC). These forms enable you to make the decision as to the type of care you plan for the end of your life. These documents should be written by a physician, certified nurse practitioner or clinical nurse specialist. It is important to discuss which DNR order is most appropriate with your doctor and attorney.

If you ever become terminally ill fall into a permanently unconscious state a DNR order would inform the emergency squad or other medical caregivers of your wish to not receive CPR, chest compressions, electric heart shock, artificial breathing tubes, and special drugs.

A DNR-CC order allows you to select the extent of treatment they would like to receive. It gives you the opportunity to reject certain treatments while still providing enough care and medication to make you comfortable as your life comes to an end. Unlike the standard DNR, the DNR-CC allows for certain treatments.

If you are able to make your own healthcare decisions, no one, including your family, guardians, or healthcare powers of attorney can override the DNR or DNR-CC. To maximize there effectiveness, it is important to provide your doctor and local hospital with copies of your DNR advance directives. You can also carry a DNR or DNR-CC identification card or bracelet stating your orders to an medical emergency squad.

A DNC order written in accordance with your doctor can be changed at any time. Nothing is set in stone. You can make changes by asking your doctor to prepare a new order. It is important to notify family members, caregivers, and any other healthcare provider that you have cancelled the old order. To avoid confusion, you should also destroy the old order and all identification cards and bracelet regarding the order.

CHAPTER 15

Caring for the Elderly

CARING FOR THE ELDERLY...

If you or your elderly family member doesn't have a doctor, contact your local hospital for names of area doctors who specialize in seniors. It is important for family members and caregivers to work with the elderly person's medical professionals to ensure proper treatment and care.

THE DOCTOR'S OFFICE

After visiting the doctor, it's important to maintain a list of the following:

- Illness diagnosis along with the dates they were diagnosed
- Causes of hospitalization along with the admission and discharge dates
- All details regarding surgeries
- Prescriptions and non-prescription taken along with dosages
- Vitamins or other supplements taken
- Specially recommended diets
- Medical equipment used (walkers, wheel chair, oxygen tank, etc.)
- Allergies
- Immunizations
- Special restrictions

THE HOSPITAL

Communication is very important when you or your loved one has been admitted to the hospital. Consider designating one person as the liaison between the patient and the rest of the family. This person would be in charge of speaking with the doctor and then relating the important information to other family members and friends.

It there is any concerns regarding hospital services, staff, or facilities, be sure to speak with one of the hospital's patient representatives. These representatives serve as advocates for patients. Medicare has its own patient advocates that can be reached at 1-800-589-7337.

MEDICAID...

Medicaid is a health program for eligible low-income people of all ages who don't have health insurance or the money to pay for medical services. Medicaid programs are based on income and medical necessity.

Each state establishes its own income and asset eligibility levels for services. In Ohio an elderly person is eligible when that person's "countable" assets fall below $1,500 and monthly expenses are less than the nursing home bill.

There are also provisions to protect the spouses of nursing home residents. Check with your Department of Human Services or call 1-800-686-1581 and ask for a bulletin called "Medicaid Questions & Answers" for more detailed information.

Keep in Mind

If you are in the hospital and have to transfer to a nursing home, Medicare will often not pay the nursing home bill if you are discharged from the hospital and return home before entering the nursing home. For Medicare to provide coverage you must be discharged directly from the hospital and sent to the nursing home. However, Medicare does not pay the whole bill; only the partial bill and for no more than 100 days.

Personal savings and Medicaid pay the bulk of nursing home bills, although those personal savings often have to be depleted before Medicaid takes over. Medicaid eligibility requires a combination of low income and very low assets.

Eligibility

There are three eligibility tests:

1. Older than 65 or disabled
2. Low income
3. Low assets

The following pages will give you a list of the information you'll need to help determine your eligibility. Remember that if you have a will you should have records to verify your assets for the past 36 months. If you have a trust the period of time to keep records is 60 months.

MEDICAID SPOUSAL IMPOVERISHMENT RULE...

One of the biggest fears senior couples have is that nursing home care will deplete their remaining savings, leaving the husband or wife still living at home penniless. Thankfully, there are provisions to protect spouses of Medicaid-assisted nursing home residents in Ohio. Some of these provisions include:

- The spouse can keep up to $2,610 of monthly income
- The spouse can keep up to half of the couple's combined assets (up to $104,400)
- An amount granted by the state to maintain minimum monthly maintenance needs.

These changes change periodically. Check with the Ohio Department of Job and Family Services or visit *www.eldercareteam.com* for more information.

NOTE...

A determination of income and assets can be complicated when a spouse is under nursing care and the other is at home. It would be wise to contact an attorney for advice before a Medicaid application is filed. For further information contact your County Department of Job and Family Services.

VERIFICATIONS NEEDED
FOR MEDICAID DETERMINATION

Remember not all of the following will be applicable for every individual.

Checklist

___ Birth Certificate
___ Social Security Card
___ Medicare Card
___ Car Title (if applicable)
___ Last three bank statements for all checking and savings accounts, stocks or bonds, certificates, etc.
___ Check registry
___ Verify life insurance policies including current face and cash value of policies and verification of policy number
___ Verify current income: SS income, pensions, union benefits, company retirement, alimony, etc.
___ Current property taxes, homeowner's insurance, mortgage
___ Additional medical insurance coverage and current premium paid monthly
___ Cemetery lot deed
___ Burial contract
___ Power of attorney papers
___ Last three years of IRS tax returns (if applicable)
___ Current rent, electric, phone, water, gas, trash bills

NOTE...

Verifications are subject to change. You may want to contact Job & Family Services in your area for a current list.

THE PASSPORT PROGRAM...

There is an option for elderly Ohioans who need frequent medical care but would prefer to live independently in their own homes. It's a Medicaid waiver program called Pre-Admission Screening System Providing Options and Resources Today, or PASSPORT. The program provides information, assessment, and medical services at home for people who would otherwise have to go to a nursing home. PASSPORT is available to people 60 years of age or older who meet certain income and health requirements.

The types of services provided under the PASSPORT program include the following:

- Meals delivered to the home
- Household chore services
- Homemaker services
- Counseling regarding nutrition
- Adult daycare outside of the home
- Social Work services
- Transportation
- Medical equipment, supplies and devices to assist a person
- Personal care assistance
- Registered nursing care
- Speech, occupation and physical therapy

Those considering the PASSPORT program can call 1-811-626-7277 to begin the application. The Ohio Department of Aging can provide further information.

ASSISTANCE IS AVAILABLE...

Home Care and Community Services

Health and social services are available in the community to help an older person live at home. Check the services you or your loved one may need.

Home Care Services

_____ Home health/personal care services like assistance with bathing, dressing and toileting
_____ Meals on Wheels
_____ Homemaker/non-medical services such meal preparation, laundry, and housekeeping
_____ In-home nursing, hospice and therapy services
_____ Telephone reassurance
_____ Home accessibility/adaptations
_____ Companionship living/shared housing
_____ Emergency response systems
_____ Medical equipment/adaptive devices
_____ Lavatory services
_____ Friendly volunteers to relieve family when older person cannot be left alone
_____ Chore services-assistance with tasks such as lawn mowing, snow removal. and repairs

Community Services

_____ Adult day care
_____ Senior Center
_____ Congregate meals
_____ Support groups (such as Alzheimer's) or other disease specific organizations
_____ Transportation/shopping services
_____ Home improvement services
_____ Geriatric assessment/care management

For those who are unable to live at home and need an assisted living facility or nursing home there are other options available.

Retirement Communities

Retirement communities offer recreation, personal security, dining rooms, and health screenings, among other accommodations. Many include a variety of living arrangements including independent, congregate, assisted living and nursing care.

Continuing Care Retirement Communities (CCRC)

CCRCs offer independent living and various health care services that last through the resident's lifetime. Residents pay an entrance fee and monthly fee and can move from one level of care to another as needed. These facilities allow residents to remain in the same community for the entirety of their lives, despite care needs.

Shared-Living Homes

These homes offer a family-like setting for older persons who are mobile and able to care for themselves. The home operator usually provides cleaning, shopping, cooking, and other minor services.

Adult Group Homes

Also known as board and care homes, these facilities generally house anywhere from six to 16 residents, providing room, board, personal assistance. They are state licensed.

Residential Care Facilities

Formally known as rest homes, these facilities are state licensed and house 17 or more unrelated individuals who need care but do not require full-time skilled nursing care. They are staffed 24 hours a day and personnel provide special diets and assistance in the administration of medication. They also help with walking, bathing, dressing, feeding, and getting in and out of bed. These facilities, however, are not qualified for Medicare or Medicaid reimbursement.

Hospice Care

Hospice care provides home healthcare for a terminally ill individual. Hospice nurses coordinate healthcare procedure in collaboration with the patient's doctor, which can be a real relief for both the patient and caregiver. Medications related to the dying process are covered under some hospice programs. The same agencies that provide regular home healthcare also have hospice programs. Medicare covers this service.

Private Duty Care

Private duty care refers to the hiring of home health aid to supervise or assist the elderly or unable with personal care, meal preparation, cleaning, and shopping. Aids are generally hired and paid by the hour. Prices can range from $15 to $25 per hour. This often allows those in need of care to remain in their homes for a longer amount of time.

Financial arrangements for any of the facilities and forms of care can vary widely depending upon location, and the forms of services and accommodations offered.

Most of these facilities charge on a monthly or yearly basis and some require a substantial entrance fee with monthly maintenance fees. Others require an endowment of assets. Costs are high because they provide substantial services tailored to the needs of the elderly.

Are you Ready to Put Your Life in Order?

NATIONAL ACADEMY OF ELDER LAW ATTORNEYS...

The following may help you to choose an attorney to assist you while planning medical decisions for an older person.

The NAELA is a professional association of attorneys concerned with improving the delivery of legal services to the elderly. Through the NAELA, attorneys exchange ideas and information on substantive elder law issues and the development of an elder law practice.

Other Academy Publications:

Questions & Answers: When Looking for an Elder Law Attorney's
Elder Law: A Practice Coming of Age

The Law & Aging Series:

- Age Discrimination
- Durable Powers of Attorneys
- Elder Abuse, Neglect and Exploitation
- Estate Planning and Probate
- Guardianship & Conservatorship
- Joint Tenancy
- Living Trusts
- Long Term Care Insurance
- Medicaid
- Medicare
- Planning for Medical Decision Making

This information was taken from the *Planning for Medical Decision Making* (2004) brochure.

SENIOR PERSONAL BIOGRAPHICAL INFORMATION

Answer if applicable and to the best of your ability.

Name_____
Address_____ City_____ State_____ Zip_____
Type of Residence_____ Home _____ Senior Complex
_____Assisted Living _____ Nursing Home
Telephone_____ Cell_____ Fax_____ Email_____
PO Box Number_____
Password(s) to Computer Files _____
Employment_____ Profession_____
Date of Birth_____ Place of Birth_____
Social Security Number_____ Location of S.S. Card_____
Martial Status: Single _ Married _ Divorced _ Widowed _Other_
Religious Affiliation_____ Church_____
In Case of Emergency person to Call_____Relationship_____
   Address_____ City_____ State_____
   Zip_____ Telephone_____ Cell_____

Family Information

Spouse/Significant Other_____
Address_____ City_____ State_____ Zip_____
Telephone_____ Cell_____ Fax_____ Email_____

Children/Stepchildren: Names, Addresses, Telephone, Cell phone numbers
_____
_____
_____
_____
_____

Siblings: Names, Address, Telephone, Cell phone numbers
_____
_____

Are you Ready to Put Your Life in Order?

_____ _____
_____ _____
_____ _____

Grandchildren: Names, Addresses, Telephone, Cell phone numbers
_____ _____
_____ _____
_____ _____
_____ _____

Great Grandchildren: Names, Addresses, Telephone, Cell phone numbers
_____ _____
_____ _____
_____ _____

Your Next of Kin_____ Relationship_____
Address_____ City_____ State_____ Zip_____
Telephone_____ Cell_____ Fax_____ Email_____

Pets _____
Veterinarian _____
    Telephone_____ Fax_____
Person designated to provide pet care _____
Special pet care instructions_____
_____

Professional Information

Accountant Name_____
Address_____ City_____ State____ Zip_____
Telephone_____ Cell_____ Fax_____ Email_____

Attorney Name_____
Address_____ City_____ State____ Zip_____
Telephone_____ Cell_____ Fax_____ Email_____

Banker Name_____
Address_____ City_____ State____ Zip_____
Telephone_____ Cell_____ Fax_____ Email_____

Dentist Name_____
Address_____ City_____ State____ Zip_____
Telephone_____ Cell_____ Fax_____ Email_____

Physician Name(s)_____
Address_____ City_____ State____ Zip_____
Telephone_____ Cell_____ Fax_____ Email_____

Hospital Name_____
Address_____ City_____ State____ Zip_____
Telephone_____ Cell_____ Fax_____ Email_____

Optometrists Name_____
Address_____ City_____ State____ Zip_____
Telephone_____ Cell_____ Fax_____ Email_____

Employer Name_____
Address_____
Telephone_____ Cell_____ Fax_____ Email_____

Financial Planner Name_____
Address_____
Telephone_____ Cell_____ Fax_____ Email_____

Insurance Company_____ Agent Name_____
Address_____
Telephone_____ Cell_____ Fax_____ Email_____
(List information for Life Insurance, Home Insurance, Vehicle Insurance, etc.)

Legal Guardian's Name_____
Address_____
Telephone_____ Cell_____ Fax_____ Email_____

Tax Preparer Company_____ Preparer Name_____

Address_____
Telephone_____ Cell_____ Fax_____ Email_____

Person named with Power of Attorney_____
Address_____
Telephone_____ Cell_____ Fax_____ Email_____

Person Named with Durable Power of Attorney_____
Address_____
Telephone_____ Cell_____ Fax_____ Email_____

Executor of Will_____
Address_____
Telephone_____ Cell_____ Fax_____ Email_____

Financial Information Income & Expenses

Banks Name_____
Address_____
Telephone_____ Cell_____ Fax_____ Email_____
Accounts: Check Number_____ Savings Number_____
           Safety Deposit Box_____Other_____

Safety Deposit Box Bank_____
Address_____

Certificates of Deposit (CD) Bank_____ Account No._____
                         Amount_____ Maturity_____
Credit Cards
Name_____ Card No._____ Expiration_____
Name_____ Card No._____ Expiration_____
Name_____ Card No._____ Expiration_____
Name_____ Card No._____ Expiration_____

Credit Union Name_____
Address_____
Telephone_____ Fax_____ Email_____

Deferred Compensation

Account Management Company_____
Telephone_____ Account No._____

Federal Reserve Bank_____

401B Account Management Co._____
             Account No._____

401C Account Management Co._____
             Account No._____

401K Account Management Co._____
             Account No._____

IRA Account Management Co. _____
             Account No._____

Joint Ownership Account Management Co._____
             Account No._____

Keogh Account Management Co._____
             Account No._____
Home Mortgage

First Mortgage_____ Second Mortgage_____
Financial Institution Name_____
   Address_____Telephone_____
   Account Number_____ Amount of Loan_____

Other _____ Financial Institution Name_____
   Address_____Telephone_____
   Account Number_____ Amount of Loan_____

Mutual Funds Management Co._____
         Address_____ Telephone_____
         Account Number_____

Are you Ready to Put Your Life in Order?

Pension

Receive Check_____ Direct Deposit_____
Amount_____ Management Co. Direct Deposit_____
Account Number_____

Savings Bonds Amount_____ Maturity_____ Location_____
Social Security Receive Check_____ Direct Deposit_____
Amount_____

Location of Important Documents

Birth Certificates and/or Bible Documenting Birth_____
Children's Birth Certificates_____
Adoption Papers_____
Baptismal Certificate(s)_____
Advance Directives_____

Citizenship Papers_____
Death Certificates_____
Deed: Cemetery Plot_____ Property_____
Other_____
Divorce Papers_____
Driver's License_____
Honorable Discharge Certificate(s)_____
Income Tax Records_____

Insurance Papers—Accident_____ Automobile_____
Credit Card_____ Health_____
Medicare_____ Medicaid_____
House_____ Life_____
Long Term Care_____ Mortgage or Loan_____
_____ Other_____

_____

Living Will_____
Marriage Certificate_____
   Pre-Nuptial Agreement_____

147

Medical Alert Card/ID_____
Organ Donor Card_____
Passport_____

Real Estate Transfer Certificate_____
Social Security Card(s)_____
Titles & Vehicle Registration Locations

Vehicles_____
Boats_____
Recreational Vehicles_____
Other Document(s)_____

Estate Planning Documents

Will Location_____
Trusts_____

WISHES AFTER DEATH

Organ Donation: Yes_____ No_____
Location (if applicable)_____

Burial

Cemetery Name_____ Plot Number_____
Address _____ Telephone_____

Funeral & Memorial Wishes

Funeral Home_____ Funeral Director_____
Address_____ Telephone_____
Cemetery Marker_____ Monument_____

Cremation

Urn's Burial Location_____
Location of Scattered Ashes_____

Type of Service (church, funeral home, etc.)_____
Memorial Service _____ Other_____

Additional Special Directions for Funeral & Memorial

Pall Bearers _____
Music_____
Poetry/Scripture to be Read_____
Speakers_____
Flower Preferences_____
Charitable Donation Destinations_____
Food Served at Memorial Service_____
Clothing/Jewelry to be Buried In_____

Items with which to be Buried/Cremated_____
Photos Displayed at Service_____
Any Other Wishes_____
_____

Attach your obituary following this document.

Chapter 16

Nursing Home Care

NURSING HOME CARE...

Entering a nursing home is often a difficult but necessary decision. Nursing facilities are for those who have physical or mental impairments that require continuous supervision and care at a skilled or intermediate level. Medicare or Medicaid generally determines the level of care needed. Nursing home placement can be on a permanent, long-term basis, but that isn't always the case. Short-term nursing care can serve as rehabilitation for people transitioning from hospitals.

Paying the costs of nursing facilities is the responsibility of the resident, although help is available when certain conditions are met. Medicare can provide financial support, however the program can only assist with the costs when the elder's medical conditions meets specific criteria set by Medicare. Even then, Medicare's coverage is limited.

If the nursing home resident runs out of money, Medicaid can offer assistance. Medicaid is offered through the County Department of Job and Family Services, but it is not accepted in all nursing homes. When you're considering nursing home placement, consult with a hospital social worker or discharge planner. The Long-Term Care Ombudsman Program is another great resource. Serving as an advocate for those in need of long term care at nursing or assisted living homes. Call 1-800-365-3112 or check the following web sight *www.1tco.org* for more information.

Chapter 17

Assisted Living

ASSISTED LIVING...

Nursing home care isn't the only option for those who need help with their day-to-day activities and would be unable to properly care for themselves in an independent environment. Assisted living is often the option for elderly people in this situation. It covers a variety of services in several different settings.

- **Campus-centered assisted living** arrangements are usually found on the grounds of a nursing home. The elderly person would live in a homelike setting and would require little or no supervision. Still the resident would have the option to participate in sponsored meals and activities.

- **Adult Care Homes**, sometimes referred to as **Group Homes**, are state-licensed private homes in the community offering care and supervision to older adults who can no longer live alone. The caretaker in these homes is generally the homeowner or a person hired by the homeowner. Each home has its own guidelines as to who they can care for. Some offer day care.

- **Assisted Living** facilities are licensed and free standing facilities that offer individual rooms or apartments for the elder. Many assistive services are offered, including meals, social activities, personal care, and more. The resident of an assisted living facility needs to be somewhat independent. Individual homes determine the elder's eligibility.

CHAPTER 18

Planning a Funeral

PLANNING A FUNERAL...

When it comes time to arrange a funeral, whether it's your own or another's, there are important decisions to make. These decisions have an impact both emotionally and financially. Depending on the choices you make, the costs can vary substantially. The following will give you an idea of the options available for funeral and memorial services as well as the expenses to consider.

Funeral Services

- Funeral Home facilities
- Ohio burial, transit, and/or cremation permit
- Professional and staff services
- Preparation of the deceased (embalming, cosmetology, hairdressing, etc.)
- Initial transfer, funeral coach, limo services
- Cremation (if desired)

Other Potential Costs

- Headstone and engraving
- Costs to open and close a gravesite
- Casket (depending on material, interior fabric, and finish, the casket can be a costly expense)
- Vault or Grave liners (as required by most cemeteries)
- Cremation urns
- Food services
- Printed memorial sets (register book, prayer cards, etc.)
- Remembrance light for placement in cemetery
- Memorial board to display personal photographs and mementos
- Audio or visual recordings of the funeral or memorial
- Flag cases to display the US flag provided for a Veteran
- Organist, vocalists, or other musical services

Obituaries

Many local newspapers will publish death notices without charge. There are fees associated with obituaries at some newspapers.

Why should you prepare for the funeral in advance?

Your Family

- Preparation spares them the emotional burden of making arrangements, allowing them time to grieve.

Costs

- Arranging early tends to reduce costs.

Securing Benefits

- There are benefits available to help pay for your funeral, as well as benefits available for survivors. Your funeral director will be able to walk you through the various benefits available, including social security, veterans aid, Medicaid, and more.

Peace of Mind

- Your family is spared from making the difficult choices necessary, and not only that, your wishes will be met in their entirety.

Contact a funeral director to guide you through the final preparations of planning your funeral.

OBITUARY

Name: _____ Age: _____

Home Residence: _____ Date of Death: _____

Place of Birth: _____ Date of Birth: _____

Occupation _____ No. of Years: _____
Date of Retirement: _____

Spouse's Name (if applicable): _____
Place Married: _____ Date Married: _____
Date of Spouse's Death: _____

Hobbies: _____
_____

Achievements: _____
_____

Name(s) of Surviving Family Members: _____
_____
_____

Name(s) of Deceased Family Members: _____
_____
_____

Funeral Home handling arrangements: _____

Calling Hours: _____
Funeral Service: _____

Memorial Donations: _____
_____

Chapter 19

In Review . . .

IN REVIEW...

Trust and Will Administration

Initial Procedures

1. Obtain and review wills, trust and codicils
2. Select and hire an attorney to assist the executor
3. Gather information

   a. Obtain death certificate.
   b. Collect personal information and papers (including financial data)
   c. Obtain names, addresses, and telephone numbers of beneficiaries and heirs

Probate the Will

1. Give notice of probate proceedings
2. Admit the will to probate court by applying to the court that handles probate matters
3. Petition the court to appoint the executor

Gathering Assets

1. Open a checking account for the estate
2. Obtain a Federal Identification Number from the IRS (Form SS-4)
3. Notify the IRS of the executor's authority over the decedent (Form 54)
4. Contact deceased's employer to obtain final paycheck and any insurance
5. Contact life insurance provider
6. Determine which assets are subject to probate and which pass automatically

   a. Joint property passes to the surviving joint tenant

b. Life insurance and retirement benefits pass to their specified beneficiaries
   c. Totten trust (payable-on-death accounts) pass to their specific beneficiaries

7. Take physical custody and control of the probate assets and safeguard them
8. Obtain valuations and appraisals of assets as necessary

Payment of Debts and Expenses

1. Pay deceased's debts (utilities, medical expenses, credit cards, etc.)
2. Pay estate expenses like court costs, executor, and attorney fees
3. File appropriate tax returns

   a. Federal estate tax return
   b. State inheritance or estate tax return
   c. Decedent's final income tax returns (Federal Form 1040 and applicable state return)
   d. Gift tax return (if deceased made substantial gifts, Form 709)
   e. Estate fiduciary income tax returns (Federal Form 1041)
   f. Trust fiduciary income tax returns (Federal Form 1041)
   g. Business and/or employment tax returns

Closing the Estate

1. Distribute assets

   a. Specific bequests of cash and/or property should be distributed
   b. Sell property in need of liquidation
   c. Establish any trusts provided in the will
   d. Distribute any remaining estate assets

2. Obtain tax clearances from appropriate government agencies
3. File final report/accounting of all receipts, disbursements, and activities of estate and executor
4. Close estate account and pay any final expenses

CHAPTER 20

Record Retention

RECORD RETENTION...

It isn't always safe to keep certain documents around Here's an idea of how long you should keep certain documents before destroying them. Paper shredders are the best way to properly dispose of these files.

Type of Documents	Amount of Time to Keep
ATM printouts	ONE MONTH after you've balanced your checkbook.
Paycheck Stubs	ONE YEAR after you've compared these with your W-2 form and annual Social Security statement
Medical Bills	ONE YEAR to see if you're able to take this deduction on your tax return. If you can, retain these documents THREE YEARS after filing taxes.
Utility Bills	ONE YEAR unless you plan to file a tax deduction. If you do, save them for THREE YEARS after filing taxes.
Canceled Checks	ONE YEAR unless being used for tax purposes. If so, save for THREE YEARS after filing taxes.
Bank Statements	ONE YEAR unless being used for tax purposes. If so, save for THREE YEARS after filing taxes.

Credit Card Receipts	ONE YEAR unless being used for tax purposes. If so, save for THREE YEARS after filing taxes.
Quarterly Investment Statements	ONE YEAR after comparing them to your annual statement.

Keep the Following Records While Active

Disability Insurance Policy	
Auto Insurance Policy	Keep to the limit of your state's statute of liability in the event there are late claims.
Homeowner's Insurance	Keep to the limit of your state's statute limitations for liability in the event there are late claims.
Health Insurance Policies	
Other Insurance document	
Loan Agreements	Keep until the loan has been paid in full and you have proof the payment has been received.
Child Support Orders	Keep until the child reaches age 21.
All Contracts	
Retirement Records and Statements	

Keep These Records Forever

- Birth certificates
- Divorce decrees
- Social Security cards
- Records of paid mortgages
- Wills
- Trust
- Death certificates
- Passport
- Marriage certificates
- Domestic partner registrations
- Adoption certificates
- Powers of attorney

Chapter 21

Resources

RESOURCES...

1. Elder Health Crisis Handbook—Geauga County Office Published by the Ohio State University, Extension
2. Senior Living Guide—Cleveland and Northeast Ohio
3. The Complete Idiot's Guide to Wills and Estates by Stephen M. Maple (Alpha Books)
4. Information from The Ohio State University Extension Estate Planning Letter Study Course
5. Information & Notes from Seminars for Estate Planning
6. Government Handbook 2005—Medicare and You and Medicare Questions & Answers
7. Department of Veterans Affairs—2008 Edition Federal Benefits for Veterans and Dependents
8. Funeral planning program from Burrs Funeral Home and Cremation Service, 116 South St., P.O. Box 165, Chardon, Ohio 44024 (April 2008)
9. Folders: 1. Planning for Medical Decision Making for National Academy of Elder Law Attorneys, Inc.
   2. Administering an Estate Without a Will from Ohio State Bar Association
   3. Do Not Resuscitate (DNR) Orders
10. Consultation with Patricia Schraff—Attorney
    Schraff & King Co., L.P.A.
    Telephone: (440) 954-9455 Fax: (440) 269-4962
    Email—*info@schraffking.com*
11. Marc Burr from Burr Funeral Home and Cremation Service
    Phone (440) 285-2182
    Email: *www.burrservice.com*

Copyright 2012